POLITICS AND LAW IN SOUTH AFRICA

Politics and Law
in South Africa

Essays on Race Relations

JULIUS LEWIN

Of the Middle Temple, Barrister-at-Law;

Advocate of the Supreme Court of South Africa;

Senior Lecturer in African Law and Administration
in the University of the Witwatersrand

London

MERLIN PRESS

FIRST PUBLISHED IN MARCH 1963

SECOND IMPRESSION JULY 1963

PUBLISHED IN THE UNITED STATES OF AMERICA BY
MONTHLY REVIEW PRESS IN 1963

By the same author:
STUDIES IN AFRICAN NATIVE LAW 1947 (BLACKWELL)

Merlin Press Limited
112 WHITFIELD STREET, LONDON W.1

PRINTED IN ENGLAND BY
Charles Birchall & Sons Ltd.
LONDON AND LIVERPOOL

FOR TWO SOUTH AFRICANS
Eleanor and Elizabeth

Contents

POLITICS AND LAW IN SOUTH AFRICA

Preface

THESE ESSAYS have in common a theme expressed in various ways. The theme is the relative power of Afrikaner nationalism, African nationalism, and English economic interests. Afrikaner nationalism has triumphed in South Africa because the only two forces that might have restrained it could not act in alliance with each other. Of these two forces, one is weak and the other strong. The weak one is African nationalism; the strong one is the old-established economic interests of the English-speaking minority who form one-third of the white people.

These two forces, although they are both opposed to the avowed aims and ulterior purposes of Afrikaner nationalism, have never made common cause against it. The basic reason why they have never done so lies in the unwavering desire of the English to carry on their mining, manufacturing, and commercial business as usual, regardless of the political consequences of their attitude. This division of forces has rendered all opposition to the Government formal and ineffective. It thus explains why Afrikaner nationalism today dominates South Africa and why the policy of *apartheid* continues to prevail, whatever its cost.

A heavy part of the cost is the increasing suspension of the rule of law.

The course of South African policy has long been clear but lately the full implications of the policy of thorough-

11

going racial segregation have also emerged. A government determined at all costs to enforce *apartheid* in the teeth of all legal or practical difficulties will abandon the rule of law itself. For the theory of human equality, which inspires the rule of law, and the theory of racial separation, which inspires the South African Government, have come into collision again and again. However the conflict may have been disguised in the past, recent events show that in the future the rule of law will continue to prevail only in the most technical sense. The deeper meaning that the term has historically borne in politics and in jurisprudence will become a thing of the past. South Africa may retain the outward forms of constitutional government, but its substance will have gone the way of its spirit, which has already departed from the scene.

These essays first appeared in recent years as articles in the journals listed on the last page of this book and I thank the editors for permission to reprint them. In a few places I have slightly revised what I wrote in order to mention subsequent events.

These essays attempt a kind of analysis which has not, to my knowledge, been made elsewhere; and I venture to hope that they may have some enduring value for those in search of a deeper understanding of race relations in South Africa.

JULIUS LEWIN

University of the Witwatersrand
Johannesburg
October 1960

I

The Balance of Forces

"We are narrowing our political and social rights. We are trying to withdraw even educational advantages from the mass of our people, who are Africans. Now that we have had our big Native wars and dispossessed the African of his land, we may get cheap labour for the mine-owners and the farmers, but we shall have created such a terrible proletariat as will be our ultimate undoing."

So OLIVE SCHREINER wrote about the Union of South Africa—in 1912 when the new self-governing state was in its infancy. In 1955, when the centenary of Olive Schreiner's birth was celebrated, her books were quoted to a generation which hardly recognized her name but which knew that her words are truer today than when she wrote them.

South Africa presents a paradox to the world. Here is a country that seems to be riper for revolution than any other, yet the years pass and nothing like a revolution occurs. Those who know the country well do not really anticipate a profound change in the coming years, unless war or slump disrupts the world. What is the explanation?

For the last thirty-five years, South Africa has been in the midst of an industrial revolution. Originally a small, feudal-agricultural colony, its economy was transformed by the discovery first of diamonds and then gold in the late nineteenth century. From the beginning, the mines were run on the cheap labour of primitive Bantu-speaking tribesmen, of whom there are now half a million in such employment. Mining dominated the economy and the politics of the country until after World War I. Then manufacturing industries sprang up and, aided by the favourable conditions presented by World War II, multiplied and prospered, and they still keep the economy expanding. Today they are the largest contributor to the national income, having outstripped even mining, but this fact is not reflected in politics. The reason why it is not must be sought in the country's dependence on gold, uranium (a by-product of gold mining), and base minerals as exports, and partly in the dependence of the many small secondary industries on the mining corporations for capital. Certainly the new industrialists have never sought to build a political party of their own. Although a mild liberalism should suit their pockets better than the unwavering conservatism of the mine owners, who look to the United Party, English-speaking businessmen are not active in politics.

The large growth of new industries has drawn to the cities two streams of wage earners entirely separated from each other by race. The one is the white Afrikaner working class now composed of skilled artisans and semi-skilled men of all types whose fathers and grandfathers were the farmers known to the world as "the Boers". (Incidentally, Afrikaners also staff all the public services, including the police force, and all government departments from top to bottom.) These men are organized in exclusively white trade unions and nine-tenths of them support the Nationalist

Party which controls the present government. The second stream of workers is the larger one of unskilled Africans on whose labour industry, like mining, rests. This class now forms about 70 per cent of those employed in industry and mining. Broadly speaking, the function of white workers, now earning a comfortable average wage of £800 a year, is to supervise and direct the efforts of black workers earning a low average wage of about £150 a year. Very few of the black workers are organized in their own trade unions, partly because they are illiterate and partly because the law refuses recognition to African unions and prevents their organization.

Both the white Afrikaner and the black African workers are at heart moved by race rather than by class. The Afrikaner has been taught, in separate Afrikaner schools, a version of South African history that makes the African his first and the British his second enemy. The "late unpleasantness" of the Anglo-Boer war and of the earlier wars with the Bantu is a tradition, like the Civil War to Southerners in the United States. The Afrikaner naturally sees in the Nationalist Party his present shield and his future hope. All the daily papers published in his language, Afrikaans, are closely controlled by the Nationalist Party. It follows that the Afrikaners are now virtually impervious to propaganda designed to wean them from their racial allegiance. For a generation or more, they have done all their thinking with their blood. No one seriously believes that political change will come in the foreseeable future through the conversion of Afrikaners to a new outlook. And, thanks to their high birth rate and their refusal to encourage immigrants from abroad, the Afrikaners number over 60 per cent of the white population, a proportion that continues to rise.

The English-speaking group numbers about a million. Since 1948, when the Nationalists came to power, this group has begun to see itself as a permanent minority unable to exercise in the future the political power it enjoyed in the past. Significantly, its United Party is now declining so obviously that its failure is noticed by everyone. Leaderless since Smuts died ten years ago, it lacks an alternative programme to the Nationalists' powerful slogan of *apartheid* or rigid racial segregation. If the United Party does not actually die (and it won't), the reason is that it holds some 30 safe urban seats in Parliament (out of a total of 156). But its survival in one form or another cannot affect the present balance of power which increasingly favours the Government under an electoral system that excludes all but white people.

Economically, however, the English middle class has prospered in commerce, industry, and mining, and they now find it convenient to take little part in politics, leaving the machinery of the state to be run by Afrikaners. Here is a curious phenomenon : the economic power wielded by the English is divorced from political power, which is entirely in Afrikaner hands. At bottom this is explicable by the satisfaction that the giant mineowners feel with a government that guarantees them a supply of cheap, migrant black labour. Moreover, the English group is influenced by the interests of Britain and the United States which have in the past provided a large part of all the non-agricultural capital invested in the country. The British interest goes right back to the opening of the mines in the nineteenth century and

16

remains strong even though capital has increasingly accumulated within South Africa, including Afrikaner capital.
The American interest is relatively recent but has risen
quickly.

From white people, there has never come any effective
opposition to the subjection of the Africans. Most of the
white voters, whether they support the Nationalist Party or
the United Party, are agreed in principle to deny advancement to Africans in every sphere. There is, however, a small
Liberal Party. Formed in 1953, this party attracted very
little support from white voters and little interest from
Africans. It has not proved viable, and the inevitable com-
promises it first made in facing white voters failed to increase
its influence. On the contrary, the white electorate declines
to support even a diluted liberal policy, however it may be
hedged around with assurances that white interests will
not thereby suffer. Whether the less liberal Progressive Party,
formed in 1959, will fare much better, is doubtful.

By now it is clear to every realist that the sole source of
effective resistance must be the ten million Africans themselves, aided by the million and a half Cape Coloured people
(descended from half-castes) and the 500,000 Indians born
in South Africa. The question that foreign observers ask is
what are the prospects of resistance from the combined
"non-Europeans" (as they are called). This is the heart of
the whole matter.

Stimulus to protest and resistance is ample enough. No
country in the world has heaped upon its people disabilities,
legal and social, so varied and intense as those suffered by
the non-Europeans of South Africa. A full list would occupy
several of these pages. It is enough to mention that Africans

17

2

have no effective political rights. They cannot live in any except strictly limited urban and rural areas, nor can they own land in any but a minute part of the country. Under the hated pass laws, they cannot move from one district to another or travel abroad without official permits. They are forbidden either by law or by white trade unions to engage in any form of skilled work. They are in effect excluded from the social services and from public amenities (including public libraries). They are prohibited from inter-marriage and even from sexual intercourse with whites. The countless laws that govern the daily lives of ordinary men and women are enforced in a fashion that makes this seem to them a police state. Every lawyer knows that an African can be arrested at any time of the day or night and the police have no difficulty in finding, after the arrest, some law under which to charge him with a crime. In consequence, the pro-portion of people in prison is higher in South Africa than in any other country.

Yet in spite of every imaginable obstacle, the Africans in the cities and towns, who now number over three million, have continued to make economic and political progress. A small middle class has emerged, although it is hardly separated from the working class. Twenty years ago, the 10 per cent of Africans who were fortunate enough to get some schooling and who were literate, had very modest political aspirations. They asked for more land, more educa-tion, freedom to move about and to trade. They hardly dared speak of political rights or to think of equality with white men. The awakening began during World War II and found expression in 1946. In that year, there was a large spontaneous strike of mine labourers on the Witwatersrand demanding a fourfold increase in the wages of 2s. 6d. a day. At the same time, the recognized leaders of the African community began to demand the repeal of all laws that embodied racial discrimination. After the Malan Government took office in 1948, the unprecedented demand for equality was first heard.

The change was not sudden. African nationalism had had a long adolescence; now it had come of age. Its education had been accelerated by the Communist Party of South Africa and, above all, by the weekly newspaper, *The Guardian,* published in Cape Town since 1937 and controlled by members of the Communist Party. This paper achieved a wider circulation than any other political weekly, especially among the non-Europeans for whom it catered. It was banned by the Malan Government in 1952 but a new paper, *Advance,* almost identical with it, appeared a week later. When *Advance* was banned in 1954, another new weekly paper, *New Age,* similar in substance and tone, appeared a week later and still continues to be published, to the chagrin of the Government which, by 1960, had not yet found a way to suppress such papers permanently.

The wartime climate of world opinion and the trend of events, first in Asia and then in Africa, also encouraged the African leaders to assert their people's claim to human rights. But the triumph of Afrikaner nationalism has finally eliminated the last hope that these rights could ever be obtained by the normal processes of constitutional government.

After 1948, the renewed pressure on Indians led them to recognize Africans as their natural allies. Possibly, too, the outlawing of the Communist Party in 1950 also removed an organization that was a potential (but hardly an actual) rival to the rather ramshackle African National Congress. Whatever the causes—and the continuous growth of industry and urbanization must be kept in mind—new forms of protest began. A united front of the African and Indian Congresses organized the astonishing campaign of passive resistance in 1952. In six months, over 8,000 men and women from these two groups "defied unjust laws". This well-organized, non-violent movement reached a climax with the adherence of a small group of white sympathizers. The Government replied with new and heavier penalties. Passive resistance to any law, however trivial, was made a serious crime punishable by years of imprisonment and by flogging, and provision was made to keep political "agitators" indefinitely in custody.

The effects of the Suppression of Communism Act were also felt at that time. "Communism" is defined in some 300 words. It includes "Marxian socialism according to the doctrines of Marx, Lenin, and Trotsky". It also includes, in effect, passive resistance and anything that might cause hostility between the white and non-white races. Even more destructive of protest was the power granted the Minister of Justice to "name" anyone who in his opinion is "a Communist", as defined in the Act. An official "Liquidator" was appointed to apply this power. He has named and listed over 500 people of all races, most (but not all) of them members of the former Communist Party. No appeal to the Supreme Court is allowed against the Liquidator's decision. Once named, a person can be ordered by the Minister to resign from his job if he holds any public office, including an office in a trade union. A number of trade

unions have lost key men and women in this way. Moreover—and this is even more fatal to the organization of
political protest—a named person can be ordered to refrain
from attending any conceivable kind of "gathering", including all political meetings, public or private. This is a punishment unique in the contemporary world. An increasing
number of persons have been prosecuted by the vigilant
political police for disobeying such orders. By this means,
the Government first crippled the African National Congress
and then suppressed it by law in 1960. The leading men
have, one after another, fallen under its ban, whether or not
they were ever Communists in the generally accepted
meaning of the term. Today what is surprising is not that
resistance has been reduced to a low ebb, but that it continues at all.

Yet it does continue. One by one, the lights are going
out as South Africa enters its darkest age. But socialists and
liberals in other countries would be proud of the unfaltering
courage and the unbroken spirit in which men of radical
mind have faced adversity. As long as this spirit survives,
resistance in one form or another will continue. It is unlikely
to take the form of physical violence, except perhaps from
limited groups, tried beyond endurance, who will be suppressed. As realists, representative African and Indian
leaders recognize that there is no means of effective resistance
to oppression while the country is ruled by a government
which wields great power quite ruthlessly The Union is the
oldest and much the strongest state in the continent of
Africa. It is equipped not only with modern arms, but also
with superior technical instruments for the control of protest
and resistance. It would therefore be foolish to imagine that

Africans are in a position to emancipate themselves shortly. Moreover, Africans still have much to learn about the arts of political organization (including wise leadership) and about the effective application of non-violent pressures. And even when they have learnt these things, they may still have to await favourable changes in the world's political circumstances, especially in Britain and the United States, before their rulers can be challenged with any hope of success.

2

The Rise of Afrikaner Nationalism

IT IS 250 years since a white man at the Cape first called himself an Afrikaner. Significantly, he was saying to a magistrate that "you can't do this to me—I am an Afrikaner". And he and his friends tried to get their own back on the magistrate at Stellenbosch who had dared to punish a white man for mere drunken disorderliness.

In the two and a half centuries that have passed since that incident occurred, the character of the Afrikaner people has remained something of a mystery not only to the outside world but even to their fellow countrymen in South Africa. The very name of "Afrikaner" was hardly ever applied to them in the world's press until their first political victory in the general election of 1948. Before that they had simply been "the Boers" who had fought gallantly in that old, unhappy war with Britain, and who remained somehow doggedly un-English in spite of all temptations to accept quietly the process of being anglicized.

The ignorance of the English-speaking world about the Afrikaners is easy to understand. There is only one book in the English language devoted to a description of this unknown nationality; it is *The Last Trek* by Sheila Patterson (1957).

Books about Afrikaners will assuredly be written in the coming years for English readers. The important position held by Afrikaners in the continent of Africa makes it certain that the world will want to know much more about them. Apart from the French left in Algeria, the Afrikaners are the only white-skinned community in the continent today who are likely to be still recognizable as a distinctive white community in the year 2000.

The political victory of the Afrikaner Nationalists in 1948 was followed by an even fuller triumph in 1953 and 1958; and no realist doubts that it will be further entrenched by the general elections in future. Political success has, however, tended to obscure the economic and social progress of this people, a fact less perceptible but no less significant. But before we pass to this aspect of their life, let us dwell for a short space on the extent of their political success.

It was not won quickly. The story goes back to the middle of the South African War. Even at that time the British themselves recognized (although the recognition was not openly announced) the necessity to come to terms with the Boers when victory was won. This recognition began when Britain abandoned the belief that a less repressive Native policy could be imposed on the Boers after the war. In the peace treaty of 1902 the British promised to postpone a decision on the vital matter of the franchise until after self-government had been conceded to the Transvaal. But before that happened the British went even further to meet the Boers' known attitude on the subject by themselves proposing in 1905 that the franchise be restricted to white men. Then in spite of warnings from W. P. Schreiner and others, the British allowed Union to come without any attempt to ensure the extension of the African franchise beyond the Cape Province. It is commonly believed that such an attempt would have wrecked the prospect of Union. But, as Keir Hardie, the Labour leader at Westminster, said at the time, "it is ridiculous to say that the great (British) trading and commercial interests whom the Act of Union will benefit—the customs and railway interests and the whole of the property interests—are going to throw away the benefits they anticipate because the House of Commons insists that the Union Parliament shall remain open to Africans, as the Cape Parliament was open".

The British surrendered one other position that was to hasten the ultimate political triumph of their enemy, the Boers. The first Governor-General in 1910 deprived John X. Merriman, the most experienced and accomplished of the available political leaders, of the office to which he was entitled, namely, that of the Union's first Prime Minister. Instead, British influence hoisted the pliable Louis Botha to that office. Botha was a modest man and (to apply Churchill's memorable phrase about Attlee) he had a great deal to be modest about. But he did have the incomparable merit of being an Afrikaner. So the political convention was at once established that the Prime Minister of the Union must be an Afrikaner. From that day to this no one has seriously challenged this convention and now it is observed by the United Party as solemnly as by the Nationalists, to whom of course it presents no problem of leadership.

Before 1948 every Cabinet consisted of English-speaking members as well as Afrikaners. Since that date the Cabinet has consisted entirely of Afrikaners. Today over 80 per cent of the members of Parliament are Afrikaners. So is the Governor-General and, almost without exception, so are the permanent heads of all the departments of State. Indeed, not only are all the key positions in the civil service held by Afrikaners but most of the minor positions are staffed by them too. The Army and the Police Force are also very largely manned by Afrikaners, who certainly predominate in all ranks. Since no informed person believes that the Nationalists will be ousted from political power in the foreseeable future, this whole situation can be called the political triumph of the Afrikaners.

It is a victory that took just about half a century to win. It was, as we have suggested, actually facilitated by the British in spite of their apparent opposition to every step in its steady accomplishment. The reason why the British can be said to have facilitated it is not hard to understand. The British interest in South Africa has always centred mainly in economic life. After all, that is where the inner substance of empire lies when all the external trimmings have fallen away. As long as the British are assured that their economic interests are in no danger, they will be extremely reluctant to quarrel, to the point of open conflict, with any country. That is why they could so generously forgive the Boers for the war that wronged the Republics so grievously.

By the irony of history, it was the South African War that led, step by step, to the domination of the Union's politics by the aggrieved Afrikaners. Ten years after the end of the war, Hertzog formed the Nationalist Party; but another forty years were to pass before it came to exercise unchallenged political power. For the party's growth was retarded by the two world wars, an embarrassing intrusion of external events on a domestic scene otherwise isolated from an unsympathetic world.

If anyone wants to inquire in more detail how the Afrikaners accomplished their political success, he will not have far to look. Dr. D. F. Malan left the pulpit in 1915 to become the first editor of the new daily newspaper in Cape Town, *Die Burger*. Dr. H. F. Verwoerd left a chair at Stellenbosch University in 1937 to become the first editor of the new daily newspaper in Johannesburg, *Die Transvaler*. A chain of other newspapers and magazines was forged around the country. With their aid several publishing firms grew up. Today few books or even articles can ever reach a sizeable number of Afrikaner readers without the approval of the Nationalist leaders, who control the production of the printed word in their language.

To make assurance doubly sure, the Nationalists and their powerful ally, the Dutch Reformed Church, captured the minds of Afrikaner youth. They did this by winning, some twenty-five years ago, official recognition for a policy that insists on the single-medium Afrikaans school as the normal type of institution for all children whose home language is not English. In these schools few teachers survive, and none are promoted, who dare to challenge the orthodox outlook bred in combination by the Dutch Reformed Church and the Nationalist Party. In these schools children are taught only the Afrikaner version of South African history. No wonder that by the voting age of eighteen (if not earlier) the younger generation is wedded to a life-long loyalty to only such Afrikaner ideals as the Church and the State choose to honour. The surprising thing is not that this happens to the vast majority of Afrikaner children; the surprising thing is that even a small proportion ever escape this fate.

It is necessary to mention the fact that some have escaped because one is inevitably reminded that Afrikaner and

Nationalist are not synonymous terms. That is true. There are still, especially among the older generation, Afrikaners who worship the names of Botha and Smuts; who recognize that all Englishmen are not (and never were, even in 1899) imperialists; and who may, at least in their hearts and consciences, question the authority of their Church on various subjects. Yet it would be an illusion to suppose that this type of Afrikaner counts for much in politics today. Their number is dwindling steadily and they are destined virtually to disappear. However hard the United Party pretends to be an alternative political home for Afrikaners, the electoral figures—coupled with the birth rate, the death rate, and the lack of immigrants—tell their inexorable tale. In any case, it is well to remember that even if the Nationalist Party split down the centre tomorrow—an improbable event—no mere realignment of existing political forces, dividing the unity of the Afrikaners, is likely to produce new national policies fundamentally different from those prevailing now.

But politics constitutes only a half (or less than a half) of public affairs. The other half goes by the name of economics.

A glance at the economic aspects of South African life helps to explain why the Afrikaners cannot relax their exertions and celebrate their political victory. They know perfectly well that political success normally rests on economic foundations. They knew this from the beginning of their Nationalist movement. They were not content to run newspapers and rely on the force of political propaganda, important as this undoubtedly was. From its early days the Nationalist Party was not simply an alternative political party; it was a broader nationalist movement of a kind whose pattern of growth is familiar to students of nationalism from a score of examples provided by the recent history of other countries in America, in Asia and in Africa, as well as in Europe in the nineteenth century. Any nationalist movement, if it is to succeed in its aims, must find expression in economic institutions complementary to its political forms. The Afrikaner Nationalists have built up such institutions. There are insurance companies, banks, building societies, nursing homes, undertakers, and a host of other large financial and commercial enterprises that have prospered greatly in the last twenty-five years. Their growth has been deliberately supported by special organizations with one eye on the main chance of commercial profit and the other eye on the indirect political value of such enterprises. This economic progress has, of course, been accelerated more recently by the fact that Afrikaners can now confidently turn to the State for practical sympathy and encouragement. Afrikaners had indeed to secure such support, in a variety of ways, before they could effectively cease to be only "Boers", as they were a century ago.

The Afrikaner middle class took a long time to emerge because it was slow to accumulate the capital necessary for further growth. And even now its economic growth is retarded by the fact that it must compete with British capital (whether from abroad or at home) holding the lion's share in several major fields of operation.

On this subject figures are difficult to come by and they come mainly (and significantly) from unofficial Afrikaner sources. According to J. L. Sadie, professor of economics at Stellenbosch University (quoted by the State Information

Office in *South African Affairs,* January 1955), the
Afrikaner share of the national income is one-quarter of the
total (which is over £2,000 million today). Apparently,
farming is still the main source of wealth for Afrikaners. In
the field of manufacturing, they own a proportion of the
smaller factories; but in mining their share is only about
$\frac{1}{2}$ per cent. Professor Sadie estimates their share of "control"
of wholesale trade to be "only 6 per cent of the total
annual turnover of £32,000,000". These few figures confirm what is known from general observation. Afrikaners
predominate in agriculture, in all the public services, and
no doubt in the lower white ranks of clerical and administrative employment generally. But in all the most profitable
fields (except farming) they play a relatively minor,
though increasing part. These include mining, insurance,
banking and finance; and the professions such as law,
medicine and the rest. Until a proper economic survey is
undertaken, a more precise analysis can hardly be made in
a reliable fashion.

Here, then, is the clue to an understanding of South
African life at the present time : political power rests entirely
in Afrikaner hands while economic power remains largely in
English hands. The English in the Union, influenced by
British capital and its outlook, are not deeply dissatisfied
with the division. Indeed, the present English adjustment
to a division on these lines continues a process that, as we
have indicated, began in the minds of the mine-owners, and
was soon legible in their policies, just after the conclusion
of the South African War. Even at that early date it was
realized that if British interests were to continue to enjoy
the fruits of their economic enterprise and investment, they

30

would be wise to avoid further conflict with Afrikaners in the political sphere. Formal opposition, in the parliamentary sense, has of course continued down to the present day. But it has grown more formal and less vigorous and purposeful as the sheer weight of Afrikaner numbers in the white population has put the outcome of political contests beyond all doubt. This division between economic and political power is a strange one, probably without parallel in another country. It is largely responsible for the continued tension between the two whites races; and this tension is one factor that prevents the ruling white race from enjoying the fulfilment of its avowed political aims.

Finally, another factor, looming ever larger in the background, must be mentioned. It is the part necessarily played by the ubiquitous non-Europeans in the economic life of the divided country. In their attitude to non-Europeans the Afrikaners can, broadly speaking, count on the support of their English fellow-countrymen on all fundamental issues. None the less, the dependence of South African society on the labour of the non-white keeps the ruling Afrikaners uneasily aware of the weakness of their own position. They have begun to realize that they now have everything under control —except the aims and aspirations of 10 million people who, while looking on Afrikaner nationalism as the root of all evil, have developed a rival nationalism of their own.

3

The Rise of African Nationalism

THE CAMPAIGN of passive resistance against unjust laws surprised everyone in 1952 by its success. Before it began no one, not even the organizers, would have predicted with confidence that it would attract such tremendous interest and support. This fact itself shows once again how white people tend to under-rate the volume and depth of feeling that moves non-whites, and how they also under-rate the steady purpose and persistence that lie behind rather weak political organization.

The illusion that white supremacy in South Africa is destined to last for ever and a day is fostered in many ways. One is the attitude to non-white organizations of the daily newspapers which provide the great majority of white people with their sole source of political information. The press seldom reports the speeches or activities of non-white leaders in any adequate fashion, and least of all when these have a constructive and statesmanlike tone. Any wild remarks or any noisy disturbance are sure of emphatic headlines. But no paper in South Africa, whether among the English dailies supporting the United Party or the Afrikaans dailies supporting the Nationalists, gave its readers intelligible accounts of the growth of the movement that reached its first climax in 1952, or rational assessments of its strength and weakness.

Yet the movement that culminated in the defiance

campaign was neither new nor sudden. Both the African National Congress and the South African Indian Congress had carried on their work for many years. Since the records of their growth and emergence into maturity are scanty, it may be useful to set down an outline of their past.

The African National Congress was started as far back as January 1912 by four African lawyers who had returned to the Union after studying abroad. The founders were Dr. P. ka I. Seme (who was connected with the royal house in Swaziland, and who died in 1951), Alfred Mangena, G. D. Montsioa, and R. W. Msimang. Dr. Seme was apparently the prime mover in the matter and he was regarded as "the father of Congress", although its first president was Rev. J. L. Dube, principal and founder of the Ohlange Training Institution in Natal. The aim was to unite the various Bantu-speaking tribes into "an African nation" to achieve political progress. The educated Africans had been hurt and disappointed by the colour bar inserted in 1909 in the constitution of the new Union of South Africa, a bar that to this day excludes them on racial grounds from ever becoming members of Parliament.

In the year after the Congress had been born, the Union Parliament, as if to stimulate the infant movement, laid upon all Africans the first of many heavy legal disabilities. The Land Act of 1913 prohibited Africans from acquiring land outside certain very limited areas that today form barely 12 per cent of the whole country. Parliament thus presented Congress with a grievance as deep and wide in its incidence as any that could have been imagined. To this day the ardent desire for more land rankles in the African mind, remaining

33

s

one of the basic causes of popular resentment against white rule.

To protest against the Land Act a deputation of African leaders went to London in 1914. As dominion status was a conception that emerged only at the end of the First World War, there was at that time perhaps some ground for hoping that Britain could and would influence the racial policy of the Union. The deputation included Dr. Dube, Dr. W. B. Rubusana (who had been elected a member of the first Cape Provincial Council, the only African ever to attain this distinction), and Sol T. Plaatje, the writer. War broke out while the deputation was in Britain and interrupted its mission. After the war, however, a second deputation was sent with the same object. It may be noted in passing that at that time, in 1919, another deputation also sought relief from Britain. It consisted of leading Afrikaner nationalists in quest of a republic independent of the Crown. Already the shape of things to come was visible. Africans were ready to appeal to opinion abroad against the Government of their own country. Many years later, after the Second World War, Africans came to look on world opinion as a source of strength in their struggle for those human rights declared by the United Nations to be desirable for all people.

In 1924 Hertzog became Prime Minister in the first Nationalist Government. Thereafter Africans were supplied with plenty of fuel to keep alive the smouldering fires of discontent. For the next dozen years Hertzog pursued his avowed aim of putting an end to the Cape liberal tradition which had allowed certain rights, including the common franchise, to Africans. After 1933 Smuts and his party joined Hertzog, and with this fusion of parties it became clear that the Nationalists' goal was in sight. The year before it was reached, with the passage of the legislation of 1936, the African National Congress itself attained a new level of organization and influence. Its conference, held as usual in Bloemfontein, in 1935, was significantly attended by some Coloured and Indian political figures. Their presence was not unwelcome to the new generation of African leaders, men with a better education and a stronger sense of political purpose than the early leaders. But opinion was seriously divided between two schools of thought. The older one, believing that half a loaf is always better than no bread, was ready to bargain with the Government in the hope that a "moderate" attitude of compromise would save some kind of rights for the future from the wreckage of past hopes. Those who held this view were faced with sharp criticism from the opposite school of thought which, rejecting compromise as cowardice, advocated non-collaboration with any official plan of "reform" and proposed to boycott any new political institutions established under it for the alleged benefit of Africans. Indian and Cape Coloured spokesmen especially were heard taking this line, new to Africans, with much force of argument and with fierce invective against those "good boys" or timid spirits who could still contemplate negotiation with Hertzog and ultimately acceptance of his major proposals.

The uncompromising view did not carry the day, but it made a lasting impression and began to divide the ranks of Africans.

Under the new law, the Native Representative Council operated for ten years from 1937. During that period, the obvious African leaders were nearly all elected to it by popular vote. Selope Thema, Dube, Godlo, Mosaka, Champion, and later Moroka, Matthews and others all played a prominent part in its proceedings; and by their side were leading tribal chiefs nominated to seats on the Council by the Government. Patiently, year after year, the Council, under the chairmanship of the permanent Secretary for Native Affairs, heard speeches and passed resolutions calling for necessary reforms in every sphere of native policy and administration. Its discussions reached a level of debate in many respects more creditable than that normal in the House of Assembly, as observers could testify. But all the eloquent words and reasonable proposals were wasted on the deaf ears of the authorities. It is difficult to recall a single important reform introduced as a result of the good advice annually tendered by this "advisory" body. No wonder that a grim sense of frustration gripped its members by 1946 when the war-time promises still remained unfulfilled. Their moderate programme of particular reforms then yielded place to a general demand that the Government abandon racial discrimination in principle and begin to grant those basic human rights of which the Charter of the United Nations had spoken so firmly. The immediate occasion for this highly significant change was the great strike of black miners on the Rand in August 1946 when the Council happened to be in session. Councillors were angered by the hostile attitude displayed by everyone in authority from Smuts, the Prime Minister, downwards, to the demands of the miners, and by the flat refusal even to open negotiations with them.

Smuts did, however, sense the change in the minds of the African leaders now united in their attitude to white authority. Late in 1947 he met some of the councillors. He offered to extend the scope of, and even grant certain limited powers to the Native Representative Council and other subordinate councils. (*Rand Daily Mail,* 14 October 1947). But this cautious and complicated plan of reform, lacking in imagination and obscure in detail, promised too little and it came too late.

In a statesmanlike analysis of the impasse, the main body of councillors rejected Smuts's rather nebulous proposals.

"In our view," said the Council in its reply, "what is required is a policy which will give the African people a sense of security in the land of their birth, a policy which is flexible and can be readily adapted to changing conditions and varying circumstances, in short a policy which recognizes that Africans are citizens of this country and not things apart.

"... General Smuts's proposals do not go to the root of the matter in dispute between the Council and the Government. The main submission of the Council has been, and continues to be, that the conditions of modern African life demand a reorientation of the whole of our native policy and not a mere tinkering with the framework of our existing native policy.

"It seems necessary to repeat the principal defects of our present native policy :

(a) It does not safeguard the legitimate rights of the African people in any aspect of their life.

(b) It holds out no hope to them of a possible change for the better in the foreseeable future.

(c) It is not calculated to integrate the African people into the general life of the country. On the contrary, it is based on the principles of permanent separatism, which engenders a spirit of hostility and racial bitterness between black and white, and as against that of mutual co-operation in the interest of both sections of the country as a whole.

(d) It is undermining the confidence of the African people in the Government of the country and is making increasingly impossible that collaboration between the Government, on the one hand, and the African people, on the other, without which no schemes intended for them can succeed." (*Rand Daily Mail,* 4 November 1947).

Even at this stage, however, the Council did not demand anything like equal citizenship or full equality with Europeans. It was still content to reiterate its main earlier proposal, the extension to the northern provinces of the limited communal system of political representation prevailing in the Cape province. But on this vital aspect of change, Smuts was silent. The Council's arguments were addressed to men with deaf ears, men already preoccupied with the exigencies of the coming general election.

A few months later Smuts lost the general election to the Nationalists. After another quarrel with the Council, the new Government did not allow it to meet again and finally abolished it, Dr. J. Moroka and Professor Z. K. Matthews having already responded to Congress pressure by resigning from it.

The Nationalists lost no time in proceeding with a different policy not only towards Africans, but towards all non-Europeans. It did not take long for Malan to begin to pass into law the policy he had preached in opposition. This policy of *apartheid* has been expounded and analysed to such an extent that it is not necessary to describe it here. It may, however, be recorded that it is Indians and Coloured people who have borne the main brunt of the recent attack. First came the Act prohibiting marriage between white and any non-white. It was followed by the Act making it a serious crime for any white and any non-white to have sexual intercourse. Then the group areas Act made possible the up-rooting of non-white traders and residents in urban and peri-urban areas where many of them and their fathers had worked and lived for generations. In a word, Indians and Coloured people were to be degraded to the status that Africans had long suffered.

No more effective method could have been designed to bring together in political unity the three communities that the Government insisted were separate racial entities, each with a distinct social life and cultural tradition of its own. True, the large Cape Coloured population remained largely unaffected by the spirit that began to animate Africans and Indians. As a community, the Coloured people had long been leaderless. Its middle-class men are nearly all teachers dependent on posts in Government service and lacking the independence of the business and professional men who lead the other racial groups.

The South African Indians, however, were more than ready to make common cause with the Africans. This they had demonstrated early in 1949 when Durban was disgraced by one of the very worst race riots in the modern history of the world. The Zulus of the city and its environs had suddenly run amok and killed and wounded hundreds of innocent Indians and looted their shops and houses, while the white authorities, slow to grasp the situation, failed for some time to curb the pogrom. With barely concealed satisfaction, the Nationalists hailed this tragedy as proof

positive of their favourite theory of inevitable racial antag-
onism between different groups. What they, in common
with nearly all white people, failed to appreciate, was the
instant and remarkable magnanimity and political wisdom
displayed by Indians after that dreadful outburst against
them. Plucking resentment and hatred from their hearts, the
Indian leaders without delay held out the hand of inter-
racial fellowship and the African leaders grasped it without
hesitation. So far from moving further apart to sulk in
enmity or to yield to despair, both groups renewed and re-
doubled their efforts to make common cause against an
oppressive Government.

The Indians had every reason to realize the necessity for
supporting the Africans. Their political status and economic
opportunities had also gone from bad to worse. First Hertzog
in 1939, then Smuts in 1943 and again in 1946 had got
Parliament to tighten the screws that supported the barriers
to their natural progress. Trading rights and residential
sites that had been held for over half a century were attacked
in a series of steady blows, both in Natal and in the
Transvaal.

A better organized and efficiently managed body, the
South African Indian Congress, had, since its inception in
1926, weathered internal storms similar to, and sometimes worse than, those that had impeded the growth
of the African National Congress. The respectable Indian
merchants represented a type of mind that was always
anxious to moderate its claims in the face of a hostile Government. Isolated and without allies in the Union, Indians
were unable to evoke even the limited degree of sympathy
sometimes shown Africans in subjection. Nor are Indians

numerous enough, or economically strong enough, to influence the Government by their own unaided pressure. In
partnership with the African National Congress, however,
they can hope to make an impact on the situation. For
Indians bring to a joint movement a riper experience of
affairs, a superior capacity for organization, more money,
and a more sophisticated outlook generally—the very elements required to make a movement of resistance into a
force no Government can safely ignore.

The Indians also brought something else of incomparable
effect. They brought a knowledge of the technique and immense value of passive resistance. It was in South Africa
before the Union that Mahatma Gandhi was first inspired
to employ this new political weapon. Gandhi spent twenty
years in Natal and the Transvaal where he first encountered
the realities of racial oppression. It was here that he devised
and practised the technique of non-violent non-co-operation.
The first generation of South African Indians was invited
and welcomed to the country from 1860. Their children
remained to suffer disabilities—legal, political, economic,
and social—that were severe fifty years ago, even if they
seem mild by comparison with those put upon all Indians
since then. For instance, the entry of Indian immigrants
was hampered even when they came to join their relatives,
and a special tax was imposed on those who entered. Indians
were prevented from living where they liked or buying
property where they pleased; and they were subjected to a
degrading system of registration. Against these and other
hardships, Gandhi organized protests. He strove by every
means in his power to persuade the authorities to rectify
obvious grievances. Patiently he negotiated with Smuts and

honourably he sought compromise on his people's claims. But having no franchise, the Indians lacked the normal instruments for political bargaining. Having no representation in the legislature, they lacked the normal means to express their opinions or to protect their interests, let alone to make the white electorate aware of their burning sense of the injustices they suffered.

In these circumstances, the novel idea of passive resistance against unjust laws came as an inspiration. Its full significance has since been the subject of study by scholars. Here it is enough to recall that in the Union's early years, *satyagraha* achieved results when nothing else did. The Indian Relief Act of 1914 lifted from Indians their worst disabilities, and Gandhi sailed away from South Africa to conquer fresh and larger fields and to win the admiration of the world by the methods of his conquest.

Those who understand the lessons of history might have foreseen that the time would come when Indians in South Africa would revive the spirit and technique of *satyagraha*. Indeed, in 1939 Jan H. Hofmeyr, remonstrating with Smuts's party against the anti-Indian law it framed in that year, warned it that Indians might be provoked to passive resistance. Before long, Dr. Y. M. Dadoo, the leader of the uncompromising radical wing in the South African Indian Congress, was actually advocating the use of passive resistance. However, he and his adherents remained a minority for years, while the so-called "moderates" sought, by appeals to reason or to law courts, to secure some modification of fresh legislation. Their efforts were of little avail. As with the Africans, successive Governments seemed determined to teach Indians the folly and futility of relying on

reason. By the time the Second World War had ended, the
Indian Congress had elected Dr. Dadoo its leader. In 1946
the newest anti-Indian laws were resisted in Natal by non-
violent non-co-operation. Nearly two thousand Indians and
a few white people, led by the Rev. Michael Scott, were put
in prison.

Meanwhile, events in the great world beyond South
Africa were moving in a new direction. Thanks to the
leadership of the greater Indian National Congress and the
inspiration of Mahatma Gandhi, India became a free state.
Taking the Charter of the United Nations at its full value,
India soon embarrassed one of its authors, Smuts, by raising
in its forum and in the hearing of the whole world, the
question of the treatment of Indians in the Union. At one
session after another the subject was debated to the disadvantage of South Africa. By 1952 the larger question of
apartheid as a policy was itself under discussion and set for
further inquiry by U.N.

Indians and Africans in the Union were encouraged by
the sympathy that their cause evoked abroad and by the
dismay that the effects of world publicity produced in the
dominant race at home. The Second World War had been
fought to overthrow the greatest racial tyranny in human
history. One of its major effects was to produce a new
awareness all the world over, and not least in South Africa,
of the evils of racialism. This bred in those most affected
by the blight a new determination to resist it in every shape
and form. Moreover, racial discrimination was condemned
repeatedly and in various ways by the United Nations. It
became wholly unacceptable, however it might be disguised,
to men who were conscious of a new freedom awaiting those

who demanded it with their old dignity supported by new contemporary forces.

Partly under the pressure of these forces, dependent status was ended in a score of African countries. Even in the colonial dependencies that remained, political rights were noticeably extended during the war and post-war period. Alone among the states of the world, South Africa chose in this same period to curtail old rights and to impose new wrongs on the majority of her people.

It was in this changing climate of world opinion that the Congress movement of the non-whites in the Union at last came of age. The pursuit by the Malan Government of its policies soon applied any sharper spur that may have been necessary. To make matters worse, European opinion failed to support Jan Hofmeyr in his efforts to make even a moderate liberalism an effective political force. Indeed, the United Party never showed real opposition to the Nationalists. Accordingly, an alternative policy to *apartheid* was never seriously put before the whole electorate. The tension of race relations grew steadily worse. In this situation one of the early casualties was the group of white liberals who had ever since the Union tended, in one way or another, to act as the spokesman of African opinion. Under the Native Representation Act of 1936, seven seats were provided in Parliament for this type of white liberal. In its early years this form of representation worked well enough, thanks largely to the fact that Europeans of unusual ability and character—notably Rheinallt Jones, Edgar Brookes, Donald Molteno and Margaret Ballinger—came forward to fill those seats. Of these only Mrs. Ballinger remained in Parliament in 1953, and she was deprived of her seat in 1960. The deep change that took place in the minds of Africans became perceptible in their attitude to this representation of black interests by white spokesmen. By 1950, if not before, Africans had lost all confidence in white liberal leadership and in the restrained and moderate policies which it presented in the face of the formidable challenge of the Nationalists.

Alone among the white Members of Parliament elected by Africans, Sam Kahn, an avowed communist, retained the warm support of an overwhelming majority of his constituents until not they, but the Government, deprived him, in May 1952, of his seat. This support was, however, not due to his communist outlook, but to his unflinching advocacy of equal rights, regardless of race, for all in South Africa, and his courageous denunciation of racialism in every form. It should be emphasized that Africans looked on him as their champion, not on communism as their cause. So much was common knowledge in the Cape, and it was confirmed by the evidence put before the parliamentary Select Committee whose revealing report (S.C.6 of 1951), by the majority Nationalist vote, recommended Mr. Kahn's expulsion from the House of Assembly. Even the English daily papers, very hostile to anything savouring of communism, could scarce forbear to cheer Mr. Kahn's performance during his three years (1949-1952) in Parliament.

There was, indeed, no good reason why Africans should any longer be content with white spokesmen. These had always held a difficult and peculiar position, in which they found themselves facing an unsympathetic European audience as often as a critical African audience. Unless, like Mr. Kahn, they abandoned all attempts to convert white opinion by a process of persuasion, a subtle change inevitably occurred in their function. They began to expound and explain, if not defend, most aspects of white policy to Africans rather than to express African opinion to Europeans.

The Indians had in 1946 rejected a similar form of communal parliamentary representation by Europeans enacted for them by Smuts, but withdrawn by Malan as soon as he took office. There were soon growing indications that Africans and Indians alike had lost interest in the ineffective efforts made on their behalf by white liberals.

The term liberal has, of course, a variety of connotations. To the Nationalists it is a word of abuse only a little weaker than "communist". Even in the ranks of the United Party, mild liberals are unwelcome and their exertions nullified by vigilant party managers. From the white electorate, therefore, there has not come the slightest encouragement to Africans and Indians to moderate their demands, to persist in patient courses, or to restrain themselves and ask for only half a loaf when pressed by their hungry followers. It has, on the contrary, been made clear that there is no real hope of political progress, however gradual, for non-Europeans.

It is this background that rendered so ludicrous the quest for "moderate leaders" among Africans that men like Mr. J. G. N. Strauss, then leader of the United Party, contemplated in 1952, after the defiance campaign had grown to a size where it could no longer be ignored. This quest failed at its outset. It failed because there *are* no moderate African leaders—if a leader is to be defined as one who has followers and is ready to "be consulted" or to negotiate with the Government or Opposition on a basis different from that adopted by the two Congresses jointly. Mr. Strauss never even got as far as actually beginning a quest, being satisfied simply to announce that if returned to office, he would consult (unnamed) moderate non-European leaders. The only effect of this line of thought was to deepen the suspicions of the Congress movement that the official Opposition would, like the Government itself, do all it could to undermine the authority of the elected Congress leaders and to weaken the position they had attained after long and difficult efforts to organize their followers. How blind to such realities white politicians remained was shown in Port Elizabeth at the time of the tragic race riots in 1952. The search for "moderates" was pursued in the very city where Dr. J. Z. Njongwe had displayed greater powers of organization and evoked wider personal loyalty than probably any other Congress leader had done to that date. The resistance campaign in the eastern Cape province obtained as much support as it did in all the rest of the country taken together. This was to be explained by two main factors. First, the African people there are more homogeneous in tribal tradition and less divided than elsewhere. They are also better educated and more Christianized after longer contact with western civilization. Resistance in this area was marked by notable religious fervour—it was often preceded by prayer—and it was supported by African clergy and by African trade unions. Secondly, the people in these parts had lost more than others since 1936 through the operation of the land and franchise laws that deprived them and their children of old-established rights.

Nor to this day do white politicians realize that the first

effect of undermining Congress was to strengthen those less responsible and less reasonable groups in African life that have begun to preach enmity against all white people as such and perhaps to toy with the idea of terrorism as a technique for securing political change. In a real sense Congress was the only alternative to terrorism, the only hand restraining Africans from demanding black supremacy as the alternative to white supremacy, the only influential voice seriously asking for inter-racial co-operation.

In the light of this record, what is surprising is not that Congress failed to formulate a detailed blue-print for progress in South Africa, or to declare itself without any ambiguity on certain concrete issues. What is surprising is that Congress continued to take a statesmanlike attitude on the large questions that present themselves for decision.

Non-white people do not want to rid South Africa of white people. Let it be stressed that only a very small minority of members of the African National Congress ever dreamed of replacing white domination with black domination. The whole bulk and weight of Congress always imagined the future of South Africa in terms of inter-racial co-operation on a basis of equality. The joint declaration adopted in July 1951, when the defiance campaign was planned, is sufficient proof of this fact :

"All people, irrespective of the national groups which they may belong to and regardless of the colour of their skin, who have made South Africa their home and who believe in the principles of democracy, are South Africans. All South Africans are entitled to live a full and free life on the basis of the fullest equality. . . .

"The struggle which the national organizations of the

48

non-European people are conducting is not directed against any race or national group. It is against the unjust laws which keep in perpetual subjection and misery vast sections of the population. It is for the transformation of conditions which will restore human dignity, equality, and freedom to every South African."

The significance of this policy, with its prospect of inter-racial peace, has been carefully obscured from recognition by any but a small element among the Europeans. The daily press of both white sections continued to pretend that Congress was essentially an anti-white movement. In fact, however, the force of the law here reinforced the wisdom of Congress. It has since 1927 been a serious criminal offence for anyone to promote hostility between the white and non-white races, and any racial indictment of white people by black speakers is liable to be punished by the courts. On the other hand, it has never been, and has not yet been, declared a crime to demand equal rights for all races. This fact is hardly understood by ordinary people. Even a Johannesburg magistrate could say in 1952 :

"It is common knowledge that one of the aims of communism is to break down race barriers and strive for equal rights for all sections of the people, and to do so without any discrimination of race, colour, or creed. It is well-known that all democracies of the world consider that communism is menacing peace and order, turning the world upside down and making stable and decent life impossible." (*The Star,* Johannesburg, 15 July 1952.)

In the mind of this magistrate, who is supposed to interpret the law of the land, the militant liberal demand for equal rights, regardless of race, is confused and equated with communism. But even under the immensely wide and vague terms of the Suppression of Communism Act of 1950, freedom to advocate racial equality is not punishable unless unlawful action towards that end is taken. Although twenty leaders of the resistance campaign were convicted by the Transvaal Supreme Court under the Act in November 1952, their guilt was held to lie in their organization of the resistance campaign, not in their advocacy of equality.

By any normally acceptable definition of "communism", the leaders of the campaign, with a few avowed exceptions, are not and never have been communists. It is necessary to emphasize this fact because continual attempts are made to smear the non-European resistance movement as nothing but "communism". Since the personalities, records, and outlook of the Congress leaders are known to only a small number of Europeans, these attempts are liable to succeed to some degree. Yet proper inquiry shows that the charge is false.

The Communist Party of South Africa was dissolved by its own act in June 1950, anticipating by a month the final passage through Parliament of the Act declaring it an unlawful body. Since the Act was passed, the promotion of any type of "communist" thought or activity has been a serious crime punishable by imprisonment. There are therefore no longer any avowed, but only former, communists. Merely to call a man a communist is defamatory, unless he has in fact been officially listed as such by "the Liquidator" appointed for the purpose under the Act.

It is, however, reasonable to ask whether the resistance leaders are communists in any ordinary meaning of the term. To answer the question, it is relevant to recall certain

50

facts unfamiliar even to the most informed people. While it was active, the Communist Party of South Africa, at least since about 1937, had always insisted on inter-racial equality and co-operation. With the possible exception of a few branches of certain Christian churches, the Party was indeed the only organization in South Africa which at that time practised as well as preached racial equality to the fullest extent. Moreover, the Party always tried to restrain African nationalism, recognizing that its political value was limited in a plural society where Africans form only two-thirds of the total population. As late as the end of 1949, the leadership and tendencies of the African National Congress gave the Communist Party much cause for sharp criticism. In a considered analysis of the political situation published in the Party's own journal, *Freedom,* (December 1949), the Party attacked the Congress and its leaders for their "bourgeois" desire to think in terms of liberal capitalism instead of communism. The analysis attributed the weakness and failure of Congress to this fundamental fault.

None the less, it must not be suggested that the Communist Party had no influence on non-Europeans. The Communist Party did contribute to African political education in one important respect. It set the pace for the African National Congress in the decade from 1937 to 1946. Its aggressive demands, its forthright propaganda, and its ably conducted weekly newspaper *The Guardian,* accelerated the rate at which Africans learnt that gradual and piecemeal reforms are unlikely to come or to make substantial changes in African status if and when they did come. The Communist Party influenced Africans—usually indirectly—to distrust moderate liberal effort on their behalf and to demand, in their own right and in a militant temper, nothing less than full racial equality in every sphere of South African life.

There is today little reason to believe that most African leaders have changed their own "bourgeois" outlook. The laws they have singled out for attack and resistance are those which hinder freedom of movement and organization, freedom to live, to trade, and to own property in any area, and freedom to participate in the common political life of the country on equal terms with Europeans. Those aims are indeed shared in theory, and sometimes supported in practice, by a number of impeccable liberals who themselves have absolutely no sympathy with real communism.

Indeed, even universal adult franchise did not become an openly emphasized aim of the African National Congress before about 1955. It was certainly not included among the avowed aims of the campaign of passive resistance in 1952. In 1955, however, a turning point was reached with the adoption of the memorable Freedom Charter that was to become a vital document in the prolonged treason trial which began in 1956.

This historic document contains echoes of the United Nations Declaration of Human Rights as well as the American Declaration of Independence. It also demanded that "mineral wealth, the banks, and monopoly industry shall be transferred to the ownership of the people as a whole; ... that the land shall be shared among those who work it; ... and that there shall be a national minimum wage."

The adoption at that juncture by the African National Congress of a broad radical programme was understandable. After 1948, when the Afrikaner Nationalists gained their first parliamentary victory, it became perfectly clear that the emerging middle class Africans had nothing to hope for by pursuing a moderate line and being ready to compromise their claims to human rights. There were, too, economic factors that accounted for the ANC's bolder attitude. Africans in the Union of South Africa had never really constituted a strong middle class. Their leaders had such occupations as preachers, teachers, clerks, journalists, and (more recently) doctors and lawyers. African business men or traders of any type are small in number to this day and were fewer still in the ranks of the ANC. These types of men can hardly be compared in economic strength with the bourgeoisie that developed in Europe (or even in West Africa in this century). The African élite in the Union represent less a rising economic interest than an emotional and intellectual revolt against restrictive laws and personal indignities resulting from the colour bar. The equality they would prefer is that which prevails in a free competitive society based on capitalism, not that in a classless society based on socialism. But because this is only an embryonic middle class, and because it has been denied all opportunities of advancement as a group distinguishable from the mass of black labourers, it has in effect been forced to throw in its lot with the working class and to make common cause with it against the disabilities imposed on all Africans as such.

The ANC thus became a broad movement embracing all Europeans, Indians, or Coloured people of mixed descent, and it carefully avoided slogans like "Africa for the Africans", which might imply a desire to substitute black supremacy for white.

This programme of inter-racial co-operation on the basis

of equality attracted support from various quarters. Hence the prevailing paradox that the stricter the law has become about race relations and free speech, the wider has grown the public interest in those very ideas about human rights and wrongs that the Government is determined to extinguish.

There is a deep irony in this fact. The Act to suppress so-called "communism" actually became an instrument that accelerated informal co-operation among like-minded people of all races who detested the Nationalists and wanted to put forward an alternative programme to save South Africa from ruin. White liberals, aggressive Christians, socialists of all shades, and, indeed, even conservatives with a social conscience have in recent years made common cause in recognizing human rights as the best basis for the reconstruction of a plural society. These diverse elements are united by their perception that Africa, like America, is not destined to remain half slave and half free.

This open alliance will continue to confront the Nationalist Government with an awkward though unacknowledged question—can the rule of law be maintained in a society built on racism? Dr. Oliver C. Cox has suggested in *Caste, Class and Race* (1948), that the rule of law and racial domination are ultimately incompatible ends. Forced to choose between them, the Afrikaner Nationalists would obviously sacrifice the rule of law. Why have they not already done so to a greater degree than they have in fact? The answer seems to lie in the solidly entrenched economic interests of the English-speaking section of the white race, who are scared of the ruling Afrikaners and who require the maintenance to some extent of the rule of law for the protection of these interests. This answer is advanced here in the belief that it may help to explain why the rule of law has not yet been suspended altogether. The question remains how far its operation will be further curtailed in the coming years. Will a Suppression of Liberalism Act be contemplated? But the trouble with such legislation would be that it would not be applauded in Washington and in London as the Suppression of Communism Act no doubt was. To attack communism in the 1950's was to be sure of encouragement and support; to attack liberalism in the 1960's would be a very different proposition. Only time can tell whether the Nationalists will undertake to do this in earnest. If they do, the historians will see the treason trial, whatever its ultimate outcome, as one stage in a course foreshadowed by the former Prime Minister, Strydom, in 1948 when he declared that

> "anyone who purposely tried to upset the Government's plan to put into operation its *apartheid* policy, or who failed to do his duty towards the realization of that aim, would be guilty of treason."

NOTE—The African National Congress (as well as the breakaway Pan-Africanist Congress) was banned by an Act of Parliament passed in 1960 during the "emergency" which lasted for five months.

4

Power, Law, and Race Relations

"THE FUNDAMENTAL concept in social science is power," writes Bertrand Russell. He goes on to say that one form of power—say, civil authority or influence on opinion or wealth—should not be studied in isolation from the others. "The laws of social dynamics are laws which can only be stated in terms of power, not in terms of this or that form of power. Power, like energy in physics, must be regarded as continually passing from any one of its forms into any other, and it should be the business of social science to seek the laws of such transformations."

Considered in this light, South Africa today can be seen in a stage of transition from the nineteenth- to the twentieth-century forms of power. The realities of the present situation are, however, obscured by the habit of the chief contestants for power, the Afrikaners and the English, of making nineteenth-century theories of law and politics their battlefield. Both sides tend to do this because in the struggle for power they both want to have "The Law" behind them and both sides argue as if The Law were some majestic arbiter, instead of recognizing law as essentially an instrument of policy in the hands of those exercising power.

In the view taken here, public law reflects an attempt to exercise political power (or to restrain opponents from exercising other forms of power). The source of law being the State, including the courts, those who want to exercise power must first gain control of the machinery of the State. Once they have done so, they can proceed to employ law as an agency of control or simply as an instrument of policy. They can be restrained or hindered only by opposition coming from the possible exercise of other forms of power than law by those who are against the purposes for which law is being used. This view of law does not deny that those who exercise power through law may be influenced to a certain degree by ethical elements, whether embodied in previous tradition or felt as a moral necessity of the times. Of course, law is in practice always subject to interpretation by the courts, which continue to perform their function because, for one thing, no parliament is able to legislate for every detail of public administration. Thus law itself comes realistically to mean, in Mr. Justice Holmes' memorable words, "nothing more pretentious than what the courts decide". Once the creative function of the judiciary is observed it is easy to appreciate better the importance attached by politicians to the personal outlook and "inarticulate major premises" of the men appointed to the bench.

Let us turn to the situation in South Africa.

Since 1948 the Union Government's policy can best be understood as fulfilling its avowed aim of making Afrikaner culture and interests dominant over (a) the English and (b) the Africans. In this task the Government has, however, encountered economic obstacles to domination over the English and legal obstacles to domination (of a different degree) over the Africans. The English—and the Africans under their influence—have tended to rely on the British nineteenth-century theory of law to support and justify their resistance to domination. "The keynote of nineteenth-century thought," say J. A. G. Griffith and H. Street in their *Principles of Administrative Law* (1952), "was individualism. Judges and politicians agreed that the maintenance of order both within and outside the country was the only 'legitimate function' of government. The causes of individualism were many : it was a reaction from the earlier feudal and Stuart rule; it harmonized with the interests of the new class of manufacturers which emerged as a result of the industrial revolution; Locke's emphasis on the sanctity of private rights and property, together with the development by Adam Smith of theories of *laissez-faire,* gave it a political philosophy; it was consonant with the Puritanical view of life. ... The emphasis of the common law was on freedom of property, freedom of contract, and freedom of the person; interferences with these freedoms were not to be countenanced."

In other words, the development of the English common law in the nineteenth century took account of the economic and social needs of the times (as C. H. S. Fifoot, among others, has well shown in *English Law and its Background,* 1932). And it was this body of law, doctrine, and precedent that was received in South Africa and has hitherto formed the basis of the judicial interpretation of questions of public law.

This fact is itself regretted by many Afrikaner lawyers, including some who have reached the bench. They are making consistent efforts to retrieve its consequences by putting Roman-Dutch law, wherever possible, in the same superior position in the field of public law (i.e. constitutional and administrative law) as it holds in the field of private law (notably family law). These efforts involve reducing the influence of English constitutional law on every occasion offered by current cases in the courts and turning to legal doctrines of the seventeenth and eighteenth centuries in the Netherlands in preference to those that prevailed in nineteenth-century England.

One major reason why Afrikaners prefer to revive an earlier legal tradition is that certain English doctrines, such as the equality of all men before the law, regardless of race, have presented obstacles to the practice of *apartheid*. Of this difficulty many examples could be supplied. A good illustration is to be found in the introduction of "separate amenities". Lawyers all knew that no subordinate authority, framing administrative regulations, could discriminate on the sole ground of race. To do so would be to act unreasonably, and since 1898 English law had clearly held that administrative regulations must not be unreasonable and this view was adopted by South African courts. In 1933 an Indian objected to the partition that had been put up to divide a Transvaal post office into two sections, one for whites, the other for blacks. There was nothing in the Post Office Act to authorize this practice; and accordingly the Transvaal Supreme Court held the regulation invalid. On appeal, however, the Appellate Division, in *Rasool's* case, 1934 A.D. decided that when equal facilities were provided for both races, it was permissible to follow the policy of separation in spite of the lack of parliamentary authority to support it. This was the law for twenty years. But by 1953 a series of cases had been won in the courts by non-Europeans who proved that the separate facilities in various public services were unequal. Accordingly, an Act was passed in that year to allow officials to provide separate amenities without the need to make them equal. Even before 1953, however, some judges were doubtful whether the rule derived from the English common law should be maintained (in spite of precedents) in the circumstances prevailing in South Africa.

Rasool's case and its sequel show how and why the Government resents English influence on the growth of law and regards it as an obstacle to the full application of *apartheid*. It may be noted that English-speaking judges (with the notable exception of Mr. Justice F. C. G. Gardiner, who dissented) formed the majority of the court in *Rasool's* case. They did not want to prevent all forms of racial separation, but they tried to ease its effects and to reconcile it with the previously established legal theory of human equality. In administrative practice, however—and no doubt because of its cost—this compromise broke down after a time when rejected and challenged by emerging Africans who wanted to assert their claim to full equality and were not content with the promise of separate but equal services.

The politicians who supported the legislation that settled the issue made their theory plain. They believe that the general election of 1953 finally confirmed the fact that *apartheid* was to be the policy of South Africa and that no obstacle and no institution should stand in its way. "If the appeal court wanted to be treated with respect," declared Mr. G. F. Froneman, himself a lawyer, in the House of Assembly on August 20, 1953, "it should give decisions interpreting the sentiments of the people who stood supreme in the country." Mr. Froneman was annoyed because in *Tayob's* case (1951 A.D.), Chief Justice Centlivres had remarked that he "did not understand a reference to public opinion (as justifying racial discrimination) or how the Supreme Court is to ascertain the opinion of the public which consists of both Europeans and non-Europeans". Unconsciously, Mr. Froneman was echoing the opinion of Mr. Dooley, an American comic character, who observed long ago that "the Supreme Court follows the election returns". To Mr. Froneman, opinions that agree with his own are "the sentiments of the people", which he wants translated into the law of the land; while Mr. Justice Cent-livres implies that there is a diversity or even a conflict of opinions, between which the Supreme Court does not want to choose. However, the court may (or may not) have been aware that an important effect of refusing to choose between conflicting opinions is usually to support the *status quo,* a result not acceptable to men bent on introducing political and social change.

At an earlier date the authors of *Muncipal Law* (first edition, 1941, page 717), Dr. T. E. Donges, now Minister of Finance, and Mr. (now Justice) L. van Winsen, in an attempt to influence the opinion of judges and lawyers, had put the matter like this: "It stands to reason that in a country whose statute book is honeycombed with differential legislation as between white and coloured, and in which colour distinctions in churches, schools, sports, places of amusement, and in society generally are carefully observed, it can scarcely be said that, in delegating legislative powers to municipalities, the legislature could not possibly have contemplated that these subordinate law-making bodies would follow its own example, as well as the settled social and colour differentiation."

In plainer language, this meant that where habits of racial

discrimination had grown up and the customs and conventions involved had been practised for a long time, the courts should recognize and adopt them as law. This view implies that "the custom of the community" is primarily the practice of the Afrikaner section of the whole population. In jurisprudence the idea that a community's custom is the true source of law goes far back. It is significant that Savigny, who defended it in the nineteenth century, tends to be preferred as an author to, say, Bentham or Austin in the Afrikaner university law schools. According to Savigny, a people's law, like its language or its moral and political order, is the product of the *Volksgeist*—of something vaguely conceived as compounded only partly of reason and primarily of instinct, custom, tradition, and authority.

As numerous cases show, South African judges have in the past been inclined to prefer a school of political thought (with its roots in the nineteenth century) that supports the *status quo* or allows only small and slow changes. By standing on precedents drawn from the century 1850 to 1950, they set themselves against rapid political or social change. Another example of this was the decision in *Harris v. Dönges,* 1952 A.D., the famous constitutional case which held that the Coloured disfranchisement *did* require a two-thirds majority in Parliament. Because the courts held up rapid change, the task of introducing it was transferred to Parliament by those who sought dominance for their opinions and policies. This accounts for the wider resort to legislation for various purposes that the Nationalists found it necessary to adopt after 1948.

The Nationalists found legislation necessary not only for the positive purpose of introducing desirable change but also for the negative purpose of resisting change undesirable from their point of view. Hence their use of legislation to prop up and reinforce the crumbling pattern of race relations, especially in the area of the personal etiquette and practice of race relations, hitherto largely untouched by law.

American scholars have studied similar tendencies in the southern states. "Law is only one of the agencies of social control," says Charles Johnson, in *The Pattern of Negro Segregation* (1944), "but it exercises the vital function of ensuring the stability and uniformity of customary practices approved by the dominant society. In a social order in which difference in race implies differences in quality and social prerogative, a legal structure defining expected behaviour in race contacts is a response on the part of the dominant group to the threat of disorganization of the traditional social order."

In South Africa recourse to law was not necessary for the control of race relations in the nineteenth century; economic forces and social sanctions were enough. These non-legal agencies of control were fully adequate for their purpose until the time when the growth of manufacturing industry brought about the urbanization of a large proportion of Africans. Then, as the Union was industrialized, the old rigid rural castes of white master and black servants or labourers became urban classes, in which social mobility was open to non-Europeans to a degree sufficient to alarm the ruling white groups.

In this situation—clearly visible in South Africa from about 1940—there emerged two schools of thought about the desirable rate of social change. They might be called the slow school and the fast school; and their reaction to the law as laid down in *Rasool's* case illustrates their differences and difficulties, in spite of their fundamental agreement about the need to maintain white supremacy.

The slow school, supported by most English-speaking people, does not like to see existing practices and institutions uprooted. Conservative in the better sense, they rely for security on tradition, precedent, and the Supreme Court. If adaptation or adjustment to a changing situation is deemed to be necessary, they rely on the slow operation of various familiar institutions (not only Parliament) to make it. Having inherited certain ideas (such as judicial integrity or civil liberties or the rule of law) from the nineteenth century, they assert the continuing validity of these ideas. They are afraid that assaults on such ideas and practices will open the door to wider social and economic changes of unlimited, unforeseeable, and possibly profound effect.

Nor is it only to legal institutions that the English have looked to retard the rate of social change. To strengthen their own position, if not to retain their previously dominant position, they have always welcomed the partial assimilation of non-English groups to English culture. But when this process proved to be difficult (as it did for Africans) or objectionable (as it did to Afrikaners) the English fell back on the social theory—hardly articulate—that two or more rival cultures, although struggling for dominance, can continue to flourish side by side on a footing of genuine equality. Such a cultural phenomenon does not seem to have existed elsewhere in modern times, certainly not where one culture was as strong as the English and the other as isolated as the Afrikaner. This view of the possibility of two equal cultures within the bosom of a single state is evidently the source of the lingering belief in the importance and value of "bilingual (white) South Africans", men who are neither Afrikaners nor Englishmen, but who somehow contrive to appreciate, if not share, both cultures. Of course, such marginal types of men do exist happily, but marginal cultures do not seem to flourish, primarily because the modern state does not foster them. A bilingual culture may be attractive in theory, but the belief in its growth does not take account of social and political realities. The theory has several weaknesses, but its fundamental defect is its failure to recognize cultural "minorities as the product of power relations" (the phrase is R. L. Schermerhorn's in *These Our People,* 1949). The notion fails to realize that where there are two or more cultures within a single political framework, one of them will sooner or later tend to dominate the others —at least under a competitive economic system like ours— even if an uneasy state of equilibrium can be maintained for a certain period of time.

The theory of two or more equal cultures has obscured the part played by culture in the struggle for political and economic power. The relation between politics and culture is indeed much better understood by the Afrikaners than by the English, mainly because it is part and parcel of a nationalist movement and the English everywhere have long found modern nationalism hard to understand.

It is the Afrikaner Nationalists who support the fast school in contrast with the slow school of thought about the rate of social change. They realized, perhaps rather belatedly, that the process of industrialization and urbanization was inevitable in South Africa. They also recognized that if the process went on it would have profound consequences for the old rural Afrikaner culture as well as for relations between white and black based on caste. Today the Nationalists see that the political power and the culture of the English no longer threaten them with domination, but that the challenge to Afrikaner power might come in the future from Africans. Hence the well-known concern to preserve the caste-like society where colour is concerned.

However, by the middle of the twentieth century it was clear that to maintain such a society in a changing world would require the co-ordination, to a large extent, of all institutions, political and social, without exception. Hence the Nationalist determination to bring all institutions—including the courts, the English universities, and even the English churches—into line with popular practice in race relations. The Nationalists see, too, that the delay in falling into line is due to the fact that such institutions, run mainly by men with a British social heritage, tend to cling to liberal political and legal theories established in the nineteenth century. Accordingly, new law must be briskly applied to compel conformity to the demands of the newly dominant culture.

The fast school has the advantage of understanding, better than does the slow school, the structure and functioning of a society in which politics, economics, and culture are all interwoven. From twentieth-century social theories practised by both fascists and communists, the fast school has learnt how a society can rapidly be transformed. There are, however, difficulties in applying the modern theories and practices of totalitarian states to South Africa. The difficulties arise from the awkward fact that South Africa is a society which includes three rooted and tough cultures, the Afrikaner, the English, and the African. The policy of making and keeping Afrikaner culture dominant in such a society accordingly meets with various types of resistance. Intellectually, the main source of resistance is ultimately the nineteenth-century liberal ideas of political and economic well-being that the English cherish; that have also influenced the Africans; and that have even affected a small but dwindling proportion of Afrikaners.

In the economic sphere this community of ideas and interest between all the subordinate nationalities—English, African, Coloured, and Indian—is clear enough. Economically, they would all prefer a society run in terms of fair and open competition, with the State playing only a negative role, holding the ring as it did, theoretically, in nineteenth-century Britain. But this limited role for the State which Afrikaners have captured at the polls does not suit the economic or cultural interests of Afrikaners because they are waging a struggle to secure not only cultural dominance but a much larger share of the national income as well.

Hitherto Afrikaners have succeeded in imposing their ideas in the sphere of politics and latterly in the sphere of law as expounded by the courts as well as enacted by Parliament. In the 1960's they are approaching the harder task of imposing their ideas in the economic sphere, with the aim of changing the existing balance of economic power at present favourable to the English group. Here they are sure to encounter stronger resistance, especially if and when they try to coax or coerce capital by law into channels of investment which it is reluctant to enter or wishes to avoid. The struggle for personal freedom in South Africa has been lost; the struggle for economic freedom is due to begin in earnest.

Because this struggle involves to some extent the interests of people abroad and connections with the economy of the western world, its outcome is at present uncertain.

It is, however, unlikely that the English can retain their present position of economic dominance or regain the position of political dominance they previously held under Smuts's leadership. As the Afrikaner Nationalists use the machinery of the State more and more to discriminate in favour of their own supporters and against all their opponents, the economic position of the English is likely to weaken, as it has already done, for instance, in the sphere of banking. The English share of control of South African society as a whole will continue to diminish while the English pursue a policy doomed to failure in the long run. This policy continues, in the face of all the evidence to the contrary, to nurse the forlorn hope of detaching from their allegiance to Afrikaner nationalism a proportion of Afrikaners sufficient to change the balance of power. Failing to understand what an influential role culture plays in politics, the English offer the Afrikaner nothing except assimilation to English culture—which he has already rejected.

It was plain by the time the South African War ended in 1902 that neither the political standards (based on nineteenth-century theories and practices) nor even the social and cultural advantages offered by the English were acceptable to most Afrikaners. To this rejection the English resigned themselves—in the face of one strong if silent consideration, namely, the powerful desire of British capital to carry on business as before, especially in the profitable field of gold-mining.

There is a parallel here between what the Northerners

did in the United States after the Civil War had brought about a temporary phase of reconstruction in the South. The political desire to put the Negroes on an equal legal footing with the white Southerners proved weaker than economic motives. Northern industrialists, eager to resume trade with the South and to hold the Southern market, wanted a policy of reconciliation to prevail. They needed social peace for their purposes and if social peace could be obtained at the price of Negro rights, this was, in their view, but a slight concession to make, as Carey McWilliams has pointed out.

In South Africa similar pressures would explain, better than anything else would, the general strategy adopted by the English from the opening of the twentieth century to the present day. The appeasement of the Afrikaners which this strategy involved was facilitated by the fact that the economic interest of the British mine-owners and of the Afrikaner farmers had one vital element in common—they both required a plentiful and continuous supply of cheap black labour. This supply, or rather the whole system of production it supported, could be assured (or so it would have seemed) only if the social status of all Africans remained low. This would explain the readiness of the English to abandon any thought of using their military victory in 1902 to impose the Cape's non-racial franchise policy on the rest of South Africa. Hence, too, the subsequent refusal of the English to seek allies, for the maintenance of nineteenth-century political (or even economic) standards, among the only people ready to make common cause with them in upholding those standards, namely, the African, Coloured, and Indian people of the Union.

It should be recognized that the liberalism of the nineteenth century was born in an environment and matured under conditions that encouraged its growth and success; and also that it contained values that endure to the present day. "It is true," writes J. Salwyn Schapiro in *Liberalism and the Challenge of Fascism* (1949, p.397), "that the bourgeois liberals aimed to advance chiefly the interests of the middle class. Yet in the process of doing so, they unwittingly and inevitably created political machinery that served wider interests; inaugurated policies that benefited the nation as a whole; and proclaimed a political and social philosophy which, in the end, was to be turned against the very class whose interests they championed. Bourgeois liberalism has the unique distinction of having created a way of life and thought that outlived the historic circumstances that had brought it forth. It was the promise of a larger liberty and of a greater equality than that envisioned by its champions in England and France during the 1830's." The development of the liberal state constituted a great achievement. As Schapiro says, a tremendous innovation in the theory and practice of government took place when, almost for the first time in history, the State became the protector of the freedom of the individual and the most efficient instrument of social progress.

In South Africa, however, the achievement of the Afrikaners has been to use the State to promote and protect the interests of Afrikaners. In contesting this policy, the English have not defended and proclaimed the universal and enduring values of liberalism. They have demanded only the continuance of economic liberalism in the sense of *laissez-faire*. Now it is precisely this part of liberal theory and practice that is hardest to uphold in a multi-racial state. Economic freedom produced a serious problem of "poor whites" or poverty-stricken Afrikaners in South Africa, a problem that was not overcome without State intervention. Moreover, economic freedom put both the Afrikaners and the Africans at a disadvantage in relation to the English who owned or controlled the bulk of capital and property, and who could also look to British capital for further support. Incidentally, the difference between the Afrikaner leaders and the African leaders lies in the fact that the Afrikaner discovered that he required the help of the State to reduce his economic inequality with the English, while the African has hardly begun to make the same discovery. Africans in the Union indeed are still inclined to cling to the outworn theory of the negative function of the State, a theory maintained and approved by the English whose interests it serves.

By the 1960's it would be clear that the English, intent on defending only their own economic interests, were destined to fail. In another generation or two their own subordinate status as a minority group would be apparent beyond any doubt and all hope of future dominance in any sphere would have been given up. Late in the twentieth century the English would have paid the full penalty for their attachment to the economics, undiluted and unreformed, of the nineteenth century.

5

The Nineteenth Century Reformer—
Dr. John Philip

T HE GREAT-GRANDFATHER of liberal thought in South
Africa was Dr. John Philip. For thirty years he was at
the centre of stormy controversy in the Cape colony.
School history books still picture him as an "interfering
missionary", itching to make mischief. But this view has been
rejected by all the latter-day English historians who, correct-
ing Theal and Cory, regard Philip as one of the few
statesmanlike figures of the nineteenth century.

This revised view is based largely but not entirely on
Philip's papers which, by a stroke of good fortune, were
entrusted in the 1920's to the right man, the historian, Professor W. M. Macmillan, himself a product of Stellenbosch
and Oxford, and the pioneer of the modern type of South
African history. Macmillan produced two books, *The Cape
Colour Problem* (1927) and *Bantu, Boer, and Briton* (1929),
which have remained the chief source of our knowledge of
Philip's life and work. It was indeed fortunate that those two
seminal books were completed without delay because by a
lamentable occurrence in 1931—the fire in the main block
(which then included the library) of the University of the
Witwatersrand—the Philip papers were all destroyed.

What kind of man was Dr. John Philip? He was born in
Scotland in 1775, the son of a weaver. His father was a man
of independence who, using a hand-loom, worked at his

72

trade in his own home, and who read and treasured the works of Swift and Bacon, Dr. Samuel Johnson and Sir Isaac Newton. At the age of 11, John, the boy with the piercing dark eyes, started work. For nearly ten years he worked at the same trade as his father but apparently outside the home, presumably in one of the new factories brought into existence by the industrial revolution. John rose to be the manager of a power mill in Dundee but, after six months in this post, he left it because he would not countenance the wretched conditions under which children were forced to work. He set up business on his own account and was soon doing well.

At this point he was caught up in the religious revival that swept through Scotland. The influential Haldane family, who were among the founders of Scottish congregationalism, noticed Philip's ability and in 1799 he went on their advice to London for three years' training for service in the church. Philip preached in the workhouses of London, gaining some experience as a minister in Berkshire, and then answered a call to Aberdeen where he remained for the next fifteen years until, in 1819, he went to the Cape at the request of the inter-denominational London Missionary Society. He had been awarded two American degrees in theology, one by Columbia and the other by Princeton University. Evidently they were honorary degrees and they were no doubt awarded because at that time English universities were not open to those outside the established church.

It is well to pause here to consider the background against which Philip had grown to maturity.

Philip's long life spanned a period of immense social changes. How tremendous these changes were can be indicated, on the political side, by two facts. In 1794, when Philip was 19 years old, treason trials were being held in Britain of men who were bold enough to demand representative government. In 1851, when Philip died, the Cape colony was itself in sight of representative government, which began three years later. Not only politics but also economic activity underwent profound change during Philip's life-time. The industrial revolution was in full swing and the transition from agriculture to industry and from domestic to factory production had widespread effects. The techniques of production were improved by new inventions, notably in the cotton and woollen industries. The process of smelting iron was perfected by the use of coal. Railways multiplied; steamships appeared; and transport was revolutionized. New systems of banking and credit put the newly accumulated capital to effective use. The population increased fast; and so did wealth.

But the status of the working classes fell and their lack of political power exposed them to the grim hardships of life in the urban factories and slums. The struggle began for political rights, for civil liberties, for the recognition of trade unions, and for minimum wages. Scotland was a country emerging from deep poverty; some parts of it were, indeed, only a couple of generations from tribal life. In his dictionary, Dr. Johnson, who disliked the Scots, defined oats as "a grain eaten by horses in England and by people in Scotland". Yet if the porridge eaten was of inferior quality, there was nothing inferior about some of the men it nourished. During the years of Philip's ministry in Aberdeen, in 1805 and again in 1812, the country was disturbed by the great strikes organized by weavers demanding a living wage. Among

74

other events of the first two decades of the nineteenth century was the battle of Waterloo which ended the wars with France. Echoes of the French revolution continued, however, to alarm the British upper classes who did their worst to crush trade unions and freedom of political discussion.

One of the great controversies of these times that must have aroused Philip's attention was that which led to the abolition in 1807 of Britain's part in the slave trade. This reform was due to the crusade organized by "the Clapham sect", that distinguished circle of allies who included Wilberforce, Macaulay, Clarkson, Sharpe, Buxton and others. The methods used by the group, says G. M. Trevelyan, "became the model for the conduct of hundreds and even thousands of other movements—political, humanitarian, social, educational—which have been and still are the chief arteries of the life-blood of modern Britain, where every man and woman with a little money, or a little public spirit, is constantly joining leagues, unions, or communities formed to agitate some question, or to finance some object, local or national. In the eighteenth century this was not so. The habits engendered by the anti-slavery movement were a main cause of the change." The Clapham sect and its allies were a formidable pressure group, as Dr. E. M. Howse has revealed in his book, *Saints in Politics* (1951). They conducted their propaganda in the form of parliamentary lobbying, press publicity, open-air meetings, and the briefing of Members of Parliament. Indeed, Trevelyan regards the success of the agitation, then unique in the character of its aims and methods, as one of the turning points in the history of the world. It led to the abolition first of the slave trade and then of slavery itself under the British flag, and thereby secured abolition by all those European nations who, in the course of the nineteenth century, divided between them the helpless bulk of Africa. Abolition came only just in time. "If slavery had not been abolished (in 1833) before the great commercial exploitation of the tropics began," says Trevelyan, "Africa would have been turned by the world's capitalists into an enormous slave-farm." It may be mentioned in passing that Trevelyan was not fully informed when he described the agitation against slavery as entirely unselfish. Dr. Eric Williams, in his later original work, *Capitalism and Slavery* (1943), has shown that some of the Clapham sect had a material interest in the East India Company which wanted to see the West Indian monopoly in the sugar trade ended. In any event, the campaign against slavery was bound to lead to re-consideration of the status of coloured people everywhere.

Another aspect of the agitation, noticed by Halevy, is of special interest to South Africans at the present day. The anti-slavery campaign was the first alliance of Christians and Rationalists, of men moved by warm evangelical emotion with men moved by cold reason, as Bentham and his disciples were. History offers few examples of so effective a combination of forces; but South Africa was to witness something similar on a smaller stage 150 years later, in the mid-twentieth century.

All this was part of the British background to the first half of Philip's life.

When Philip came to the Cape in 1819, he must surely have brought with him a sound knowledge of how to apply pressure in order to secure changes in public policy in the days before Parliament at Westminster was responsive to an electorate and before the Cape colony had a legislature at all.

In Cape Town Philip at once stood out as a man of exceptional ability. He was indeed a popular figure—until he began to champion the cause of the Coloured people. Philip was quick to realize that missionary work, if it was to have enduring effects, depended on schooling for the Cape Coloured children. He believed that schools should precede churches. The experience of mission stations had shown that improvement was possible and practicable for the Coloured people. But, as he noted, "nine out of ten farmers are opposed to education for the Coloureds". (It may be noted that at this date there was little primary education for the common people in Britain.) Here lay the roots of conflict. The white colonists, as Philip also observed, wanted cheap labour. To their minds the status of the Hottentots was so close to that of slaves that it was hard to distinguish from slavery.

Philip himself did not lack sympathy for the frontier farmers in their losses and sufferings at the hands of the Hottentots and the Bantu who were inclined to satisfy their own basic needs by whatever means they could. Conflict arose because Philip was attempting to gain recognition for standards of conduct and welfare that were only then dawning in Britain. His desire to see proper measures for security adopted was strengthened by his knowledge of what was really happening on the frontier and beyond. Thanks to his long journeys and tours of the interior—which he continued regularly until he was 70 years old—Philip knew more and saw farther ahead than anyone else. He also kept up correspondence with other missionaries—Americans in Natal,

77

the French in Basutoland and others—to whom he had from the outset of their enterprises acted as adviser and friend. Philip was in fact very well-informed, but occasionally he was misled by an informant and sometimes his own indignation may have clouded his better judgment in particular cases where ill-treatment of Hottentots was alleged against a farmer. Philip's critics have made the most of instances of exaggeration or minor mistakes of fact on his part that led to bitter controversy. (The fullest exposition in English of the view that Philip was just a mischief-maker is to be found in the officially published Archives Year-book for South African History, Vol. 1, 1940, pages 93-253, in a long article by C. E. G. Schutte on "Dr. John Philip's Observations regarding the Hottentots".)

Yet it is part of Philip's distinction that he was never content merely to expose particular cases of atrocities in race relations. In contrast with the isolation of the farmers, Philip's wide knowledge of the whole situation enabled him to understand and led him to condemn the system that prevailed more than the men who were entangled in it.

Here is an illustration of the sort of argument that occurred, an argument with a contemporary South African flavour.

Towards the end of his life, Philip, on tour near Basutoland, encountered a party of farmers who had trekked from the Cape colony. He recognized one of them, a man who, he records, had earlier said : "I must trek because Dr. Philip has spoiled the Hottentots. Dr. Philip has got a law passed which would compel me to marry my daughter to a Hottentot. I would rather shoot her than see her so degraded. Dr. Philip also took all my slaves from me. I wonder at the mercy of

God in suffering such a man to live." None the less, a long and friendly talk took place on that occasion between Philip and the farmers. Science not politics was the main subject, it appears, because Philip noted that he (who had read Newton) failed to convince the farmers that the earth was not flat!

The quality of Philip's mind and the nature of his aims is best shown by quotation from the remarkable book that he wrote in the course of his first eight years at the Cape. Published in two volumes of 450 pages each in London in 1828, it was entitled *Researches in South Africa.*

"Expostulate with many farmers of South Africa for excluding their slaves and Hottentots from their places of worship and denying them the means of instruction," wrote Philip, "and they will tell you at once that they are an inferior race of beings. (Yet) we are all born savages, whether we are brought into the world in the populous city or in the lonely desert. It is the discipline of education, and the circumstances under which we are placed, which create the difference between the rude barbarian and the polished citizen, the listless savage and the man of commercial enterprise, the man of the woods and the literary recluse. By the present condition of the Native tribes of South Africa we may see what our own ancestors were like at the time Julius Caesar invaded Britain. The character of a people depends on the influence of the laws and government under which they live. When the inhabitants of this free country are heard justifying the injuries inflicted on the Natives of Africa, or opposing the introduction of liberal institutions among any class of them—on the vulgar grounds that they are an inferior class of beings to us—it is but fair to remind them

that there was a period when Cicero considered their own
ancestors to be unfit to be employed as slaves in the house of
a Roman citizen." (In a footnote, Philip quotes from a letter
to Atticus in which Cicero wrote : "Do not obtain your slaves
from Britain. The English are stupid and utterly incapable
of being taught. You will find none of them with any literary
talent.")

"It is only under a free government that the human mind,
like a tree planted in generous soil, attains to its full growth
and proportions. It is where men are governed by equal
laws; where government becomes regular and stands on the
basis of regular institutions; where rulers are under salutary
checks; where the population is raised above the chilling influence of penury; where they have peace to cultivate and
reap their fields—it is under these conditions that the march
of the human mind is unimpeded. . ."

He adds that "at our missionary schools you will see the
young Hottentot, the Bushman's child, the young Kaffirs,
their countenances beaming with intelligence, surpassing the
children of the colonists in their school exercises."

What did Philip want for the Coloured people?

Firstly, he wanted the pass laws and the offence of
vagrancy to be abolished. Secondly, he wanted them (in his
own words, perhaps echoing Adam Smith whose *Wealth of
Nations* he may well have read) to "have the right to sell
their labour in the best market". Thirdly, he wanted them
to have the opportunity to acquire education from the
Christian missions and land from the Government. Fourthly,
and above all, he wanted free persons of colour to have
equality with Europeans in the eyes of the law. This last
aim was achieved, at least formally, by the famous Ordin-

ance No. 50 of 1828, which was not only passed in the colony but entrenched by law in London against repeal, save with the consent of the British Government—a precaution, added with the aid of the Clapham sect, that turned out to be very necessary.

Knowing that the white colonists had often simply taken land where and when they could, Philip wanted the Government to set aside some land for Coloured people, as was done in 1829 with the Kat River settlement. When this experiment had been under way for a short while, Philip wrote to Buxton that it "presented a scene of industry, sobriety, and decency unsurpassed by the peasantry of any country in Europe". This was confirmed by Colonel Bell, the Government Secretary, who said that "those settled at Kat River as small farmers have made surprising progress". (Quoted in the *Memoirs of Thomas Fowell Buxton,* 1848. Everyman edition, pages 108 and 109.)

After 1830, when, as Philip believed, the legal status of the Coloured people was finally assured, he turned his attention to the plight of the Africans. What did he want for them? Firstly, he wanted to see them protected against invasion and encroachment by white farmers who were apt to dispossess them of land and cattle. Secondly, he wanted to see the geographical separation of black and white. Those who to this day vilify Philip ought really to honour him as one of the earliest advocates of segregation, at a time, before the Great Trek, when this policy was still practicable. Thirdly, Philip wanted to see the rule of law and order on the frontier. He realized, long before anyone else did, that this condition could be maintained only by a police force of some kind, and that it meant putting an end to the commando system.

81

This system took various forms but, broadly speaking, it involved enforcing the *spoor* law. Commandos of farmers or soldiers or both were authorized to cross the frontier in pursuit of stolen cattle. They followed the *spoor* to a kraal and seized the cattle or an equivalent number. If they failed in this purpose, they returned later in stronger force and, as a reprisal, took as many cattle from the Africans as they pleased. This method of dealing with stock theft kept the frontier restless and unsettled, until it was abolished in 1834 after the sixth frontier war. It was no substitute for magistrates and a police force, which Philip proposed but which was not organized until twenty years later, after two more frontier wars had caused terrible devastation and havoc. Philip saw that the problem of keeping order on the frontier was not simply a military problem and he pleaded for an ordered society under the rule of law. He also saw—and said—that it was not only stock theft that had produced the commando system but the increasing demand by farmers for cheap labour, a demand which could not be satisfied as long as the Africans had their own land and cattle to support them.

Professor Macmillan's final considered view is this :

"Of Philip's personal share in all these things, it may now be said that all the evidence finally contradicts the tradition that Dr. Philip had a meddlesome itch for 'intrigue' and interference. At a great many points his intervention was important and effective. But in every instance he delayed, usually till the scandal was too great to permit him to keep silent, always till he had first-hand knowledge on which to base his representations. The first example of his delay was in taking up the battle for Hottentot rights. A second concerned the eastern frontier. His first serious tour was in 1830, his first official letter was written only in March 1834 when a crisis was imminent. About the Trek itself he kept almost complete silence till after his tour of investigation in 1842 ... Till the breakdown in his health in 1845, when he was seventy years old, he continued to confine himself to the question of the moment which concerned the Griquas and the Basuto, most unfortunately giving little or no attention to the administration of the other treaties."

Not the least of Philip's penetrating insights was into the necessity of providing education for those whom missionaries hoped to convert to Christianity. In the course of a very long letter to an American correspondent—first published in 1833 in the *Missionary Herald* in Boston—Philip gave an exposition of his views on "the natural capacity of the African race". The whole letter is one of the most important documents Philip ever wrote. In the course of it he said : "Because multitudes in England and America have lost their religion—to which they are indebted for their civilization—many pious people make light of civilization as connected with the labours of missionaries. But it should never be lost sight of that, although men may retain their civilization after they have lost their religion, there can be no religion in such a country as this without civilization; and that religion can have no permanent abode among us if that civilization does not shoot up into regular and good government." (The letter occupies sixteen pages in *The Letters of American Missionaries,* edited by D. J. Kotze, van Riebeeck Society, Cape Town, 1950.)

Looking back, one can of course see that Philip, like nearly all Victorians, under-estimated the force and tenacity of non-European custom and culture, especially in the pattern of family life. He was no doubt also mistaken in thinking that individual tenure of land would solve the economic problems of peasants. No one in Philip's day did foresee the deeper difficulties that the process of westernization of non-Europeans would reveal. Yet Philip was enough of a realist even in these things to say: "The romantics have exaggerated the virtues of the Natives . . . Between the world of the European and the world of the Native, there is a great gulf."

Philip died in 1851 and was buried alongside the old mission house at Hankey, near Port Elizabeth. Twice in recent years his grave has been desecrated by vandals whose only knowledge of his work was no doubt derived from history as taught in nearly all the schools. Nowhere in South Africa is there a memorial worthy of Philip. Yet if one wishes to see his monument, it is only necessary to look around. The missionary tradition has fallen on hard times in these days. Yet it would be almost impossible to find a single African or Coloured man of any distinction who did not owe his early education to a Christian mission. The shortcomings and errors of judgment of the missions can be freely recognized and are indeed admitted by them. Yet it may well be questioned whether the present Government which has now taken over their function of education, will make a better job of it.

Looking back, one can also perceive the weaknesses inherent in a situation that left to immigrant Christians, who were relative new-comers to the country, almost the entire burden of responsibility for the welfare of Africans. In race relations in the nineteenth century that was perhaps inevitable. Missionaries were the only men who worked with and spoke up for Africans. And it was because they did so that, in the twentieth century, it has been possible for a broader alliance of public-spirited white South Africans—Christians and others, as in the anti-slavery crusade—to carry on the tradition of altruistic service not to one racial group or another but to a common society.

More than that: the questions, moral and material, that Philip raised in his time—education, the pass laws, land, the separation of races, the rule of law in race relations—were still alive at the end of the nineteenth century, fifty years after his death. These persistent questions, in recognizably similar form, can be traced down to the controversies of the present day. It is a sombre thought how little the basic issues in race relations have changed from Philip's day to ours.

One notable change, however, there has occurred in the last decade or two. African and Coloured people today no longer need Europeans (whether missionaries or others) to speak up on their behalf. Politically, they have come of age and can speak for themselves, thanks to the march of education and the different climate of opinion in a changing world. To appreciate this change, it is necessary to remember the work of the forerunners, among whom Dr. John Philip is entitled to a pre-eminent place. His memory deserves to be cherished by all who carry on the work begun by a brave and gifted pioneer.

6

Sex, Colour and the Law

ONE VITAL feature of South Africa's policy of
apartheid is known to have failed—the attempt to
prohibit by law sex relations between the races. So
vital is this feature that critics of prevailing policy have long
been accustomed to the inevitable question put by their
opponents : "Would you like your sister to marry a Native?"

Those who do not reply with an emphatic negative are
regarded as beyond the pale of normal controversy. Not only
opposition to any form of social equality, but also the reten-
tion of innumerable legal disabilities in the political and
economic spheres, is ultimately defended by pointing to the
disaster of social and sexual equality that would otherwise
overtake the country. What Myrdal found in the southern
part of the United States and recorded in *'The American
Dilemma'*, is true of South Africa, if one looks beneath the
surface of any argument—sex is the hidden principle, at
least in popular theory, around which the whole structure
of *apartheid* is organized.

It has not always been so. The arguments against social
equality are no doubt old, though they have hardly ever
been explicitly discussed in the large literature on race relations in South Africa. What is relatively new is the resort to
law to ensure that a powerful aversion which is supposed to
exist in cultural theory shall be maintained in actual
practice.

Sex, Colour and the Law

Looking back, one finds that the first attempt to legislate on the subject of sexual *apartheid* seems to have been made early in this century, soon after the close of the South African War, in all four British Colonies (as they then were). A Cape law passed in 1902 was adopted in the Transvaal, the Orange Free State and Natal in 1903, when a similar ordinance was applied to all three of those territories. The Cape law simply prohibited under a severe penalty intercourse between consenting adult persons "for the purpose of gain", if the woman was white and the man black (but not between white men and black women). In the Transvaal and Natal the reference to gain, i.e. money, was omitted. The enactment of this double moral standard is in line with British colonial tradition, which passed similar laws in Rhodesia and Kenya and no doubt elsewhere, laws generally repealed or amended only in recent years.

The immediate reason why the British introduced this law into South Africa was evidently the arrival of prostitutes from Britain on the Rand during the Boer War. Although they meant to cater for the British soldiers, the prostitutes found clients among Africans, a situation that must have alarmed all who believed that if the sex barrier collapsed, other colour bars would not survive.

The main idea behind the law, however, was the one still found in the American South and described by Myrdal. It is that whereas sex relations between white men and black women affect only the Negro race, sex relations between white women and black men "would be like an attempt to pour Negro blood into the white race". The reasoning runs like this: the child of a black woman by a white father would be regarded as black (regardless of its actual colour);

whereas the child of a white woman by a black father would pass as white and thus dilute the purity of "white blood".

Whatever the mythology, it should be noted that when Afrikaner governments came later to legislate on the subject, they abandoned the double moral standard upheld by British laws. Oddly enough, for nearly three centuries after white settlement had taken root at the Cape, the Afrikaners made no effort to curb miscegenation by law. This attitude cannot be explained by the absence of inter-racial intercourse, as the present-day existence of one and a half million Cape Coloured people sufficiently testifies.

How extensive miscegenation was in the seventeenth, eighteenth and nineteenth centuries, it is hard to say. Once the process had been established, people of mixed descent would, of course, reproduce themselves and so enlarge the coloured population. But there can be no doubt that miscegenation did take place on a considerable scale long before social theory and political pressure combined to render it unmentionable.

The first "Immorality Act" against sexual intercourse (but not against inter-marriage) between Europeans and Africans was passed by the first Nationalist Government in 1927. The well-known politician, Tielman Roos, who was Minister of Justice at the time, spoke of requests for legislation he had received from white women's organizations; and he recalled that several commissions of inquiry had objected to the double moral standard reflected in the earlier laws enacted by the British before Union in 1910. Unlike the British, however, the Nationalists aimed to treat both races and sexes alike; they "wanted to protect black women from white men" as well as white women from black men. More-

over, Tielman Roos had no objection to inter-marriage between the races. Although he noted with satisfaction that the
law in the Transvaal had never allowed such marriages—
by simply making no administrative provision for them to
take place—he added that Transvalers could cross the
boundary, get married in another province, and then return
to live, quite legally, in the Transvaal.

For the next ten years the subject was not apparently
debated in Parliament, although one cannot be sure because
Hansard omits the key word—"immorality"—from its
index. Nor was much heard of it in the press, except for an
occasional report of a case brought before the courts. By
1937, however, the situation of the rival political parties had
changed. The "purified" Nationalists under Malan's leadership by then formed the official opposition; and—probably
to forestall them—General J. J. Pienaar, who supported the
Hertzog Government, introduced a private member's Bill
to extend the legal prohibition against intercourse with
Africans to inter-marriage with them. Among others, J.
H. Hofmeyr, the liberal Cabinet Minister, opposed this
measure, contending that it was unnecessary to apply law
to prevent something, admittedly undesirable, against which
strong social sanctions anyhow existed. As the Government
did not allow time for the Bill to proceed, it was never voted
upon and fell away.

Miscegenation was, however, an awkward subject for an
uneasy coalition, and Hertzog gained time by appointing a
Commission of Inquiry. Its Report on mixed marriages,
published in 1939, recommended the Transvaal evasion of
the direct issue by providing different administrative regulations for marriages between two white persons and between

89

two non-white persons, but making no provision at all for inter-racial marriages. This should be done "without the use of language or expression which might give offence to any race or persons".

One of the two women members of this Commission, Mrs. N. B. Spilhaus—an old Cape liberal—expressed dissenting opinions. She quoted figures to show that marriages between black and white had since 1925 numbered less than one per cent of all marriages and had decreased to four per thousand. "Colour," she remarked, "had been infiltrating into the white population since the seventeenth century, with no visibly bad results in the descendants of the families in which it is present."

The Commission was asked to consider inter-marriage only, but it perceived—what Tielman Roos had somehow failed to realize ten years earlier—that if the problem was defined as miscegenation, or sex relations across the colour line, it would be necessary to prohibit intercourse as well as inter-marriage; and that, of the two, the former was the wider "social evil".

Being an enlightened person, Mrs. Spilhaus shrank from tackling this "evil" by law, foreseeing that "armies of detectives, police, and night-watchmen" would be required for its enforcement. She also realized, if dimly, that there was more than one problem, since she doubted "that the class of persons who indulge in immoral intercourse will be easily driven into marriage" (with an African), as Tielman Roos had supposed. The Commission did not even consider extending the proposed law to the Cape Coloured people.

The outbreak of the Second World War postponed further debate on the question. It also led to Hertzog's downfall and put Smuts in office, with Hofmeyr in an influential position, for the next eight years. By the time that period was drawing to a close, Malan's party was conducting an election campaign on various issues, of which one was the menace of miscegenation and the necessity for new laws to combat it.

The Malan Government, taking office in 1948, promptly carried out this part of its programme. In 1949, marriage between white and *any* non-white persons was firmly prohibited; and in 1950, sexual intercourse outside marriage was likewise prohibited if one person was white and the other "coloured", a term defined very broadly so as to include the Cape Coloured people and Asians as well as Africans. In 1957, the Strydom Government went still further and made it a criminal offence to commit in private "any immoral or indecent act", if one person was white and the other coloured (but not if both were white or both coloured).

This last amendment to the law was designed to make it much easier for the police to secure convictions in cases (which were common enough) where actual or attempted intercourse was hard to prove. The difficulty of proof was anticipated by the 1939 Commission, which suggested a rule of law declaring "proof of the existence of certain circumstances shall be deemed to be *prima facie* evidence of intercourse, e.g. that the parties were living together for a period, or were occupying the same room at night, or were discovered in a state of undress, or in such circumstances as would naturally lead to the inference that illicit sexual relations had taken place, or were about to take place".

After the new Act was passed in 1957, however, it was enough for the prosecution to show that one of the accused had attempted or invited or incited the commission of an (undefined) indecent act. It is the application of this Section 16 of the Immorality Act of 1957 which has produced the spate of prosecutions reported in the daily newspapers in rising numbers during the last couple of years. By 1960 it was known that over 300 cases had been heard every year since 1951 in the magistrates' courts in all parts of the country. This means that one person is prosecuted on every working day on which the courts sit. Incidentally, in their eagerness to prosecute, the police (like the 1939 Commission quoted above) have lost sight of the important distinction between stable and lasting relationships, involving families with children, and casual incidents resembling prostitution. The term miscegenation is used by those in authority to cover both these very different kinds of human relations.

In 1959 the daily press was disturbed by the extent of miscegenation disclosed in court cases. Some of these cases made news; for among the accused in various provinces since 1957 were a *predikant,* a headmaster of a school, a well-known attorney, wealthy farmers who were married men, and the secretary to the late Prime Minister—all men whose social status was much higher than that of the men normally accused. From some cases it could be inferred that the police received help from informers; but even so, a senior police officer has admitted that only a very small proportion of all the offenders against the law are discovered.

The situation revealed is a curious commentary on the attitude to *apartheid* of an unknown number of white men; and especially of Afrikaners, who admittedly form a high percentage of the men brought to court.

The leaders of the Afrikaner community are themselves

somewhat at a loss to explain, or to explain away, the situation. Of course, their debates, seldom in public, are influenced by the preconceptions of the powerful Dutch Reformed Church about sexual morality in general and by its anxiety about the deterioration of Afrikaner family life in the urban environment. The Government itself is now confronted by an awkward situation. The penalty for miscegenation is imprisonment, usually for six months, without the option of a fine. The possible maximum term of imprisonment has been increased to seven years since legislation was first passed, but heavier punishment has obviously not had the desired effect. No Government will repeal the existing laws. To hide the Afrikaners' "shame", a new law allowing the press to publish only the initials, not the full names, of accused people was considered by the Department of Justice.

The Dutch Reformed Church has obviously discovered that the Afrikaners' interest in sex has increased, is increasing, and ought to be diminished.

It is significant that the Immorality Act of 1957 also tightened the law affecting brothels and prostitution; and from recent cases in the courts, the police are known to have increased their zeal in combating these forms of unlawful activity. What has hardly been perceived, however, is the probable relation between miscegenation and prostitution. There is reason to believe that before 1950, the majority of professional prostitutes came from the ranks of non-white women. In the Cape Province these would have been attractive Coloured women, and elsewhere African women newly emancipated from tribal restraints and newly introduced to the arts of cosmetics and fashionable dress.

After the law had tried to cut off this supply by making

all intercourse with non-white women a serious crime, it seems probable that the demand for prostitutes, known in almost every port and big city in the world, has been met in South Africa by a certain class of white women, including Afrikaners.

The first Immorality Act was passed in the 1920's, the years when industrialism and urbanization first began their rapid growth; and renewed efforts were made to extend the law in the 1930's, when the same economic and social processes had gone further and made a wider impact on all races of the population. No city in the western world claims to have rid itself of prostitutes or to have solved the moral and social problems implied by their continued existence. No one should therefore be surprised to find that Cape Town, Durban, or Johannesburg has a similar problem, perhaps aggravated by racial factors. It seems probable that, when sex relations with non-white women were penalized some white women were exposed to temptations which seldom came their way previously.

Yet even these assumptions do not account for the whole situation. The rising number of immorality cases heard in the courts do not come only, or even mainly, from the cities and bigger towns. Records show that cases are heard all over the country, including the smaller *dorps,* where professional prostitution seems unlikely ever to have flourished. Moreover, miscegenation is not the same thing as prostitution, which implies payment to the woman for her services. To judge by the press reports, evidence of payment by the white man is lacking in some (perhaps many) cases, possibly because it is not necessary for the police to prove payment in order to secure a conviction. Nor would an unsolicited payment, made on a single occasion, necessarily stamp the woman as a prostitute within the normal meaning of that term. In the kind of case which is commonest nowadays, the police have merely to produce some evidence from which it can be inferred that overtures to intercourse were made.

It would seem that in order to understand the sexual attraction which black women have for some white men, it would be necessary to inquire beyond the sexual demand supplied by prostitutes in other countries. It would be necessary to know something of the special white mythology about the enjoyment of sex across the colour line, which is known to exist in the American South and which may exist also in South Africa.

One other aspect of the question may be touched on. Although there is no evidence to support their view, some Nationalists appear to believe that it is the liberals with their emphasis on human rights and their desire for social contact between the races, who are likely "to go too far" and indulge in miscegenation. In January 1959, for example, the Minister of Bantu Administration asked the City Council of Johannesburg to agree to prohibit a dozen white citizens (whose names were given) from receiving Africans as visitors in their homes (a prohibition possible under another law passed in 1957). Nationalist newspapers, supporting the ban contemplated by the Minister, were quick to hint that social contact would or could lead, among other things, to contravention of the Immorality Act. It seems that some Nationalists think about these things in the terms Abraham Lincoln spoke of when he once "protested against the counterfeit logic which presumes that because I do not want a Negro woman for a slave, I do necessarily want her for a wife".

(Lincoln himself was "horrified by the thought of the mixing of blood by the white and black races".)

The Nationalists hate any kind of informal social contact between white and non-white people. Not content with avoiding such contact themselves, they want to prohibit others from having it. One way of preventing it is to imply that such contact inevitably leads to miscegenation. And, of course, the mere threat of prosecution under the immorality laws would be enough to deter most men from inter-racial contact with women, because a prosecution, reported in the press, is enough to ruin a man's reputation, even if it ends in his acquittal.

That this is not a fanciful idea is perfectly illustrated by a case heard in 1959 in a Cape Town court. The only evidence against a white bus driver charged with immorality was that he had been found playing cards late at night with a Coloured family. A member of the family testified that they had helped the accused when he was down and out, giving him food and ironing his shirts. Acquitting the accused, the magistrate advised him to break off his friendship with the Coloured family. "For a white man to have social contact with non-Europeans," he said, "is to run a very grave risk."

Amid the new forms of statutory immorality created by South African law, the true nature of morality is forgotten. True morality in sex relations, as Bertrand Russell has pointed out, consists essentially of respect for the woman and unwillingness to use her solely as a means of personal gratification without regard to her own desires. In this light one can see how improbable it is that positive respect for human rights and proper recognition of social equality between races and sexes, would lead to those very casual sex relations across the colour line which form the bases of criminal charges.

For the men typically convicted of statutory immorality are not liberals openly preaching the importance of racial equality. On the contrary, they are men caught in a web of racially prejudiced thought and action; for it is precisely those who habitually treat non-white people as tools to be used for the white man's convenience, who find it natural to use black women for a passing sexual purpose.

From most of the cases reported in the press, this conclusion is clear : miscegenation arises out of the whole system of racial inequality, out of the popular habit of regarding all non-white people as essentially inferior, and out of contempt for "lesser breeds without the law".

7

7

Public Policy Never Changes

THE NEED for a racial policy common to all parts of South Africa was felt long before Union in 1910. Within two years of the end of the Anglo-Boer War a commission was sitting to discuss the question. Appointed by Milner, nine of the eleven men who sat on this commission were English-speaking and of British origin.

The policy they sketched in their Report, published in 1905, is, in its essential features, recognizably the same policy as the one that prevails today. The limitation on the ownership of land by Africans; the pass laws; the fear of a common non-racial franchise and the alternative of communal political representation; the design of employing the tribal chiefs for administrative control—all these salient purposes were approved at that distant date.

When Hertzog was in search of a Native policy twenty years later, some of his advisers must surely have known this Report of the Inter-Colonial Commission and drawn their main ideas from its pages. Looking back, a writer in the conservative imperial journal, *The Round Table,* in 1932 perceived that the Report was "mainly the natural product of well-to-do land and mine-owners, representatives of an acquisitive society hardened by pioneering experience and eager for economic development".

This insight accounts for what is otherwise mysterious about the passing of the first Native Land Act as early as

1913. Why were such severe restrictions put at that time on the freedom of the Africans to acquire land, even by proper purchase? No convincing excuse was made in Parliament. A minor reason may have been the recent legal transfer to Africans of land that they already occupied but were not allowed to own in the Transvaal until the decision by the Supreme Court in *Tsewu's* case in 1905. This adjustment did not increase the actual amount of land in African hands but it may have led Europeans to believe that the amount was rapidly increasing.

A more substantial reason was no doubt the serious difficulties that the mine-owners of the Rand had long faced in their unending quest for a veritable army of unskilled labourers willing to work for very low wages. This chronic shortage was indeed one of the factors that had impaired the relations between the Transvaal Republic and the *uitlanders* and led to the Boer War. The mine-owners knew from their experience the relation between land and labour. If the Africans were free to acquire more land, they would be reluctant to leave the reserves to work for low wages in the mines, and the constant shortage of labour would get worse. It may well be surmised that, behind the scenes if not openly, there was pressure on the Government to close the door against this possibility. The first Prime Minister of the Union, Botha, was amenable to the demands of the mine-owners. In 1903 he said that "he would, if necessary, break up the reserves (including the Protectorates) in order to provide labour for the mines and farms".

Whatever the pressure for its passage, the Land Act was a heavy blow to the Africans, coming as it did three years after the new Constitution itself had excluded them from ever sitting in the Union Parliament.

Like all South African affairs, colour policy is affected by events abroad. The First World War occupied public attention from 1914 until 1919 and its economic aftermath explains the next phase of policy. The generally unsettled situation, coupled with the high cost of living and the lack of economic planning, threatened the standards of the white working class. Moreover, the effects of the Land Act were now felt in the reserves where the population was increasing but not the area of land available to it. The interests of the mining industry had already been further safeguarded in 1911 by the legislation dealing with the recruitment of labour. Under this law a colour bar against the use of Africans in skilled or even semi-skilled jobs had long operated at the request of the white miners, and it was strengthened when their trade union was first recognized by the mine-owners in 1915. A crisis began some years later when the Transvaal Supreme Court held the regulation embodying the colour bar to be *ultra vires*. The price of gold was falling and so the mine-owners were tempted to seize the opportunity provided by the disappearance of the regulation to employ fewer white men and more black men at a lower wage and also to let the black men do semi-skilled work. It was this policy that precipitated the great disturbances which ended in civil war on the Rand in 1922.

The white miners lost the decisive battles but in the end they won the political campaign that followed. Smuts's Government fell from office in 1924 and Hertzog lost no time in entrenching the colour bar by the Act of 1926.

Later it became apparent that this struggle, and its out-

100

come, had been the turning point in Native policy; it remains the most significant event since Union. What was
really decided by the explosion of 1922 was that white public
opinion would never tolerate the replacement of white labour
by black labour at a lower wage. The crisis made a deep
impact not only on the public mind but on the mine-owners.
They learnt the lesson that a permanent part of the cost of
mining in South Africa was the acceptance of the colour
bar. Never again did they attempt to abolish, or even to
lower, racial barriers on the mines. From that time the mine-
owners and the white miners entered a kind of partnership
based on a common attitude denying advancement to
Africans in the industry.

The pattern of partnership thus established in the
country's biggest industry was followed, in one way or another, in the secondary industries that began in the 1920's,
flourished in the 1940's, and were still growing in the 1950's.
Industrial relations were firmly shaped by the Act of 1924,
which remained almost unaltered until it was tightened to
the detriment of white trade unions in 1956. The vital feature of this legislation was the exclusion of Africans from
trade unions. Another Act of 1953 attempted to provide
separate machinery for the settlement of industrial disputes
involving Africans. But what kept the status of Africans in
industry low was not only these laws but the inherent weakness of the illiterate and the unskilled class of labourers, a
weakness aggravated by the pass laws and the laws governing
urban areas.

The expansion of the Union's economy between the two
world wars drew from the countryside and into the towns
two streams of men, one white, the other black, in search of

work and wages. This second historic great trek of the Afrikaners continued for more than twenty years before the peak was passed and the white population stabilized in the proportion of less than half-a-million, or one-sixth of the total, in the countryside. The parallel trek of the Africans began after (if not during) the First World War and continues to this day, in spite of numerous and increasingly harsh laws designed to stop it. The census taken in 1960 revealed that over one-third of the ten million Africans are now resident in urban and peri-urban areas.

Europeans, including the Afrikaners, have accepted the inevitable fact of urbanization as it affects themselves, but pre-conceived ideas about African policy, coupled with sheer blind prejudice have prevented them from accepting the same fact as it affects Africans. It is this failure that lies behind all the urban-areas legislation passed since the Smuts Government introduced the first Act in 1923. Few things are more astonishing than the persistence, through nearly forty years, of the same rigid framework to "control the influx" of Africans, a migration compelled in fact by the economic pressures in the reserves much more than by the economic and social attractions of the towns. The historian of the future will surely comment on the blind refusal of white opinion to recognize that restrictions and even political penalties have not proved stronger than the economic forces responsible for industrialization and its sequel, urbanization.

The historian will not have to look far to confirm the theory that ideas can possess men. During the nineteenth century, if not before, ideas about Africans became fixed to such a degree that hard facts to the contrary could not shake them. One of these stereotyped ideas was the notion that, in times of social change, it was possible to employ the unchanging institution of tribal chieftainship as an efficient element in Native administration.

The British had developed first the practice and then the theory of this form of "indirect rule" in India, in West Africa, and later in all their African dependencies. By 1927 when this technique of local and regional government attracted Hertzog's attention, it had grown to be an orthodox and unchallenged feature of British colonial policy. The Native Affairs Department in Pretoria had for at least ten years been toying with the idea of granting the tribal chiefs ampler recognition and of allowing traditional Native law and custom to play a bigger part in the administration of justice. The acceptance of this idea by politicians was retarded only by the recollection that the chiefs had in earlier generations been the natural leaders of the resistance to conquest and white supremacy. It was this idea that eventually inspired the important Native Administration Act of 1927, a framework for tribal government that anticipated the first Bantu Authorities Act of 1951. (Incidentally, what no one in South Africa seemed to notice was that by 1939 British colonial policy had begun seriously to modify indirect rule, recognizing its obvious shortcomings when faced with the challenge of democratic pressures.)

There are unconscious factors that explain why the Union made the attempt after 1927, and vigorously renewed it after 1948, to revive tribal institutions in obvious decay. To the mind of Europeans, nothing marks Africans as a different race with a different culture so clearly as the survival of Bantu customs that have no place in western culture. Indeed, to stamp this primitive culture as "different" is itself a relatively recent courtesy; for generations it has been frankly looked down on as inferior and not merely different, in the sense that French culture is different from English. Why are Europeans determined to preserve "Bantu culture", even against the wishes or the true interests of the Africans themselves? The real reason is, as Dr. Oliver C. Cox has pointed out, that Bantu culture marks all Africans as a people apart, unfit to assimilate the standards and values of the richly "civilized" Europeans. It follows that the standards and means by which white men shape their relations with other white men need not be applied to black people. In plain words, in order to exploit Africans fully, it is necessary to disguise the process by professing to have a deep respect for their peculiar culture. By this means Europeans hide even from themselves the consequences of dispossessing Africans of their lands and forcing them to work for low wages in enterprises highly profitable to white people. Behind all the specious concern shown by Europeans for "the soul of the Bantu" under the protection of tribal institutions and Native customs lies the white man's own desire to rationalize the economic subjection that he has imposed on the Africans.

Land, labour, and the theory of tribal institutions—it is the inter-play of these three factors that explains, more than anything else, the evolution of African policy since the close of the South African War. The mine-owners and the farmers have long shared a permanent need common to all big employers, the chronic need, somehow or other, to find enough labourers at a wage low enough to enable their mines and farms to show a substantial profit. It is this need for cheap labour that also explains the first appearance of pass laws a century before Union. It is this need that explains the steady maintenance of the pass laws as rules of the game in which farmers and mine-owners compete for the available supply of labour.

Once this fundamental fact is grasped, the contents of the statute book since Union take on a monotonous appearance. Whatever the annual variations, the theme continues essentially unchanged. The more that colour policy seems to change, the more it has remained the same. Fifty years ago men were solemnly discussing "the Native problem"; they are still debating it today with the aid of a richer variety of masked words that yet fail to obscure the grim economic realities behind all the political verbiage.

However, this does not mean that nothing in the Union has changed in the field of race relations during the last fifty years. Significant change has indeed come, but not in Native policy or in the white man's outlook on it. What has changed is the black man and his attitude to white men. When the British proposed in 1905, to limit the franchise in the Transvaal (then a British colony) to white men, no black man's voice was raised in protest. By 1909, however, the colour bar in the Union's constitution did not pass without protest from African leaders who dreamed that one day their sons might sit in Parliament. The African National Congress was formed in 1912, and in the following year the first Land Act presented it with a second major grievance on which to grow. The Congress movement grew slowly but its growth was eventually quickened by the new climate of opinion in race relations produced by the Second World War. By 1946 the liberal Cabinet Minister Jan Hofmeyr, was surprised by the demand put forward by African leaders for the repeal of all laws involving racial discrimination. By 1952 hundreds

105

7*

of thousands of Africans had learnt from their Indian fellow-countrymen and political allies the force of passive resistance. By 1956 no African aspiring to leadership would dare to accept a programme for his people based on anything less than essential equality. That is why no African organization murmured a protest when in 1959 the meagre and useless form of communal representation of Africans in the Union Parliament was abolished. For by that time the white man's unchanging ideas about Native policy were no longer of close concern to those who endured the policy. Africans were thinking about their own destiny in very different terms, confident they would one day march by a different route towards a clearer goal.

8

No Revolution Round the Corner

VISITORS FROM abroad, and even some who know the country well, often ask "how long can it go on". By "it" they mean the present state of the Union. They are always surprised if told that there is no reason why "it" should not go on almost indefinitely and certainly for a good many years. People who think otherwise talk in terms of an impending "explosion". When you press them for a clearer idea of what that word really means, you soon find that it implies a revolution of some sort.

The belief that a revolution is due to occur in South Africa sooner or later is derived from the political circumstances that have developed since 1948. Before that date it seemed to most people that, however bad conditions in the country were for the majority of the people—the Africans—slight improvements were made from time to time, and these gave hope for the future. When the Nationalists came to power, however, they set about closing all the doors that had kept open the possibilities of change. What is more, it was soon made plain that the Nationalists did not want progressive change, however small and slow, to occur; on the contrary, they were determined to subdue everything that might promote social change in the direction taken by the rest of Africa and the rest of the world. The previous policy of amelioration was displaced by the new policy of regimentation. Moreover, the new rulers of the Union took steps to make

107

it impossible for any political party or, indeed, any political organization to get the present policy reversed fundamentally by ordinary constitutional means.

Once people realize that public policy cannot be altered in the traditional way, their thoughts turn to unusual methods of making their opinions heard. Hence the use of the term "extra-parliamentary methods". It is used, rather vaguely perhaps, to indicate the publicity value of strikes, popular demonstrations, processions, and similar techniques of protest. In recent times, the Torch Commando and the (white) Black Sash movement were respectable examples of such attempts to make protest effective by means other than putting up candidates to contest elections. Although such methods of protest were new to Europeans, Africans have long had to rely on them. But since 1958, protests and even processions, always hard enough to organize, have, generally speaking, become unlawful except by permission of the authorities, who often prefer to prohibit them altogether.

Knowing or feeling all this, social reformers have despaired of seeing any real changes in the total situation. That is why they keep on asking when the revolutionary explosion will occur.

Behind this question there is a simple idea that revolutions just happen when the time is ripe. The serious study made of the subject by Professor Crane Brinton, the Harvard historian, in *The Anatomy of Revolution* (Vintage edition, 1957) should disillusion those who hold this idea in their heads. The historical fact of the matter is that certain well-defined circumstances have to be present in combination before an attempt at revolution is likely to succeed.

Let us look at the conclusion drawn by Professor Brinton

from his study of the four famous revolutions—the English one in the seventeenth century, the American and the French in the eighteenth, and the Russian in the twentieth. Different as these obviously were in time and circumstance, Brinton shows that they all had certain features in common. Let us see what they were and then ask whether comparable conditions prevail in South Africa.

First, all four countries were on the upgrade economically before the revolution came. The revolutionary movements originated in the discontents of fairly prosperous people who felt restraint, cramp, annoyance, rather than downright crushing oppression. (This description applies broadly to most Africans in the Union.) Certainly, Brinton says, these four historic revolutions were not started by down-and-outers, by starving, miserable people. The revolutionaries were not worms turning, but men of hope with a philosophy behind them.

Secondly, we find in these societies, in the years before each revolution, very bitter class antagonisms of a rather complicated kind. It is not simply a case of feudal nobility against bourgeoisie in 1640, 1776, and 1789, or of bourgeoisie against working class in 1917. The strongest feelings seem to have been generated in the hearts of men—and women—who had made money, or at least who had made enough to live on, and who contemplated bitterly the barriers presented by a socially privileged aristocracy. Revolutions seem more likely when social classes are fairly close together than when they are far apart. "Untouchables" very rarely revolt against a God-given aristocracy, and Haiti gives one of the few examples of successful slave revolutions. This agrees with the fact that in South Africa the loudest rumblings of discontent do not come from farm labourers, or even peasants in the Reserves, but from the African middle class —such as it is—and the urban working class, who are better off than their rural cousins.

Thirdly, the machinery of government in all four countries was inefficient. This was due partly to neglect and partly to a failure to make changes in old institutions. New conditions, arising from economic expansion and the growth of new monied classes, new ways of transport, and new business methods, laid an intolerable strain on governmental machinery adapted to simpler, more primitive conditions. This last point best shows us where South African circumstances differ materially from those prevailing at the time of the four historic revolutions that seem to provide parallels.

To start with, the machinery of government in South Africa is not, on the whole, inefficient. Inefficiency in this context must surely imply much more than the administrative deficiences which are a common source of public irritation. Indeed, since the vital machinery is manned almost exclusively by Afrikaners in sympathy with the Government and its policies, it is more reliable in its operations—from the Nationalist point of view—than it would be in the hands of a different set of civil servants, whose greater technical efficiency would be offset by their political neutrality or opposition.

This point acquires special importance in relation to the control of the armed forces. Brinton finds that "no government has ever fallen before revolutionists until it has lost control over its armed forces or lost the ability to use them effectively; and, conversely, no revolutionists have ever succeeded until they have got a predominance of effective

110

armed force on their side. This holds true from spears and arrows to machine guns and gas". Brinton is also aware that the loyalty of the armed forces could be a crucial factor in a revolutionary situation. He says "that the nowadays common view that modern weapons have for the future made street risings impossible is probably wrong. Even modern weapons have to be used by police or soldiers, who may still be subverted".

But that view is not wrong when applied to South Africa. Not only have non-Europeans no access to modern weapons and training in their use, but the loyalty of the men who do handle such weapons is of a different quality from that found outside Africa. The attitude of white soldiers and policemen towards non-Europeans is notorious. No realist believes that the loyalty of the men in the armed forces is open to subversion, least of all in a racial crisis. It follows that the race riots that occur periodically are inevitably localized and therefore subdued without much difficulty. Least of all in so large a country with such poor communications as South Africa can rioting spread and grow into a revolution.

In any case, it is important to distinguish revolution from disorder. As Brinton himself admits, "disorder in some sense appears to be endemic in all societies and certainly in our Western society. The historian turned diagnostician can find evidence of disorders and discontents in almost any society he chooses to study. If a stable or healthy society is defined as one in which there are no expressions of discontent with the government or with existing institutions, in which no laws are ever broken, then there are no stable or healthy societies. A normal or healthy society will not be one in which there are no criticisms of the government or the ruling class, no gloomy sermons on the moral decay of the times, no Utopian dreams of a better world around the corner, no strikes, no lock-outs, no unemployment, no crime waves, no attacks on civil liberties. All we can expect of what we may call a healthy society is that there should be no striking excess of such tensions; and perhaps also that most people should behave as if they felt that, with all its faults, the society were a going concern. Then we may look about for the kind of signs just described—discontents expressed in words or deeds—and try to estimate their seriousness."

Our contention is that the signs of discontent in South Africa, when all added up, do not amount to a serious situation in the sense of a prelude to revolution. For one thing, the long-continued economic prosperity, which is shared to a significant extent by Africans, and the rising standards of living generally, tend to compensate people for the sense of personal frustration induced by colour bars. In South Africa today most people do still behave as if they felt that, with all its weaknesses, the country were a going concern. Only a small minority think otherwise, and even their actions commonly belie their fears.

When the visitor from overseas is persuaded that there will be no revolution tomorrow, he turns to another possibility. Surely, he argues, the non-Europeans have already learnt how to use the moral force of passive resistance. The campaign of 1952 and the stay-at-home strike on the Rand on 26 June 1957 (and in previous years) indicate the future trend. If this trend continues—so it is argued—the Africans, assisted by Indians and even by Coloured people, will sooner or later be able to paralyse the country and so force concessions from the Government.

There are two points to be answered here : one concerns the effectiveness of a general campaign of passive resistance and the other the effect of strikes by workers in particular industries.

The experience of 1952 offered only limited encouragement to those who put their faith in passive resistance. The campaign lasted from June 26 until it reached its climax on December 8, when a small band of Europeans led by Patrick Duncan "defied an unjust law" by entering the Germiston location without permits. In all, more than 8,000 non-Europeans were sent to jail for short terms. It is commonly believed that the campaign was killed by the ferocious new Acts of Parliament passed in February 1953. The fact of the matter, however, is that the campaign had showed signs of waning late in November 1952, and the Congresses really made a virtue of necessity by calling it off some weeks later, after the climax had been reached. One has no desire to belittle the courage displayed or the hardships endured by those who courted punishment in those fateful months. But facts are stubborn things, and the fact is that at no time did the campaign shake—though it did anger—the Government; nor does anyone who was wide awake in that period honestly think that it ever looked like producing anything remotely resembling a truly revolutionary situation. Since that time the severe new laws, passed as a direct result of the campaign, have sufficed to suppress any inclination to organize another campaign on similar lines. It is one thing to go to prison for two weeks and another to go for two years and to be flogged in addition.

There remains the other question, whether strikes in particular industries can become general enough and last long enough to wring major concessions from any South African Government. Only those who have never been close to trade unions imagine that it is an easy matter either to organize aggressive trade unions or to lead them into strikes for a political purpose. The idea of trade unionism is over thirty years old among Africans in the Union. It goes back to Kadalie's day, the mid-nineteen-twenties. This is not the place to discuss why Africans are so slow and so ineffective in organizing trade unions. But when every allowance is made for illiteracy and other obstacles, such as hostile laws, the fact remains that Africans have made comparatively little headway in the last generation in this field of endeavour.

Moreover, even if trade unions were much stronger and more wisely led, it is difficult to see what vital industries or essential services could be brought to a standstill. If and when urban Africans did strike in large numbers, their place would be taken and their work carried on somehow by White workers or by other Africans brought, if necessary, from neighbouring territories where Africans are more backward and much less politically conscious than they are in the Union. Add to this the fact that African workers predominate in hardly any service or industry where temporary stoppage or slowing down would at once create a national crisis impossible to resolve. The gold mining industry is not such an industry. Even if it were, the experience of August 1946 showed how a strike could be dealt with and terminated within a week or two.

The events of 1958 and of the "emergency" in 1960 confirm this conclusion. The various reasons for failure are not relevant here. What is significant, however, is that official arrangements were made on a high level in 1958 to prevent the breakdown of essential services. These arrangements were planned by an inter-departmental committee, headed by the Secretary for Labour and representing the Union Defence Forces, the police, the prisons, and the Department of Native Affairs. Nothing is gained by forming opinions on the basis of illusions; and it is an illusion to suppose that South Africa, so obviously rotten with injustice, must be ripe for revolution. Yet the last word need not strike an entirely hopeless note. The view that change will not come in the foreseeable future by reason of an "explosion" of a revolutionary character does not imply that no changes at all are possible in the status and condition of Africans. How and when they will eventually come, no one can foretell. But in Thomas Hardy's words, "if way to the better there is, it exacts a full look at the worst".

Acknowledgment

1   From Monthly Review (New York), 1955.

2   From Africa South (Cape Town), 1956.

3   From The Political Quarterly (London), 1953 and
    Monthly Review 1958.

4   From The Political Quarterly, 1959.

5   From Race Relations Journal (Johannesburg), 1960.

6   From Africa South, 1960.

7   From The Political Quarterly, 1957.

8   From Africa South, 1958.